Choosing your
A Levels

AND OTHER POST-16 OPTIONS

Choosing your A Levels

AND OTHER POST-16 OPTIONS

3rd Edition

Gary Woodward

Choosing your A levels & other post-16 options

This third edition published in 2008 by Trotman Publishing, a division of Crimson Publishing Ltd., Westminster House, Kew Road, Richmond, Surrey TW9 2ND

© Trotman Publishing 2008

First and second editions published by Trotman and Co Ltd in 2005, 2006

Author Gary Woodward

British Library Cataloguing in Publication Data
A catalogue record for this book is available from the British Library

ISBN 978-1-84455-163-7

Typeset by Newgen Imaging Systems Pvt Ltd.
Printed and bound in Great Britain at TJ International, Padstow, Cornwall

Contents

PART ONE: OPTIONS AND DECISIONS

PART TWO: DIRECTORY OF SUBJECTS

PART THREE: EXAMS AND BEYOND

About the author

Gary Woodward is an independent career management consultant and careers writer. He has written many articles for careers magazines and websites, as well as for national newspapers. He has significant experience of advising young people on job-hunting strategies as well as helping more experienced career professionals with their career development. He is also the author of the book *Winning job-hunting strategies for first-time job-hunters.*

Acknowledgements

Thanks to Neil Roscoe for sharing his insights into the post-16 education sector.

Glossary of terms and abbreviations

Term/abbreviation	Definition
ACCAC	Qualifications, Curriculum and Assessment Authority for Wales
AQA	Assessment and Qualifications Alliance. One of the five main exam boards in the UK
A levels	Advanced levels
AEA	Advanced Extension Awards. These are for candidates who want to reach an exceptional standard in their subjects
AS levels	Advanced Subsidiary levels (forming half of a full A level, but a qualification in its own right)
A2	Advanced level – the second half of a full A level
BA	Bachelor of Arts degree
BEd	Bachelor of Education degree
BEng	Bachelor of Engineering degree
BMus	Bachelor of Music degree
BSc	Bachelor Science degree
CCEA	Council for Curriculum Education and Assessment (Exam Board in Northern Ireland)
Diploma	Usually lasts one or two years and is often related to a specific area of work. Can be taken after a Level 3 qualification or at postgraduate level
Edexcel	One of the three main exam boards in England
FdA	Foundation degree (Arts)
FdSc	Foundation degree (Science)
Fieldwork/Field trip	Practical activities related to subject of study that happen away from school or college, often outdoors. Such as a visit to a site of archaeological importance
Foundation degree	This lasts two years part-time and is a combination of study and work experience. Can be converted to an Honours degree or used to go onto specific areas of employment
Gap year	A year out, often taken between school and university or between graduation and starting a career
GCE	General Certificate of Education

Apprenticeships	A way for young people to train while working in particular skilled areas
NVQ	National Vocational Qualifications
OCR	Oxford, Cambridge and Royal Society of Arts Examining Board
PGCE	Postgraduate Certificate in Education (a requirement for most trainee teachers)
QCA	Qualifications and Curriculum Authority
Sandwich course	A degree course which includes a year working as part of it
Specification	An outline of the course of study produced by exam boards. Previously called a syllabus
SQA	Scottish Qualifications Authority
UCAS	Universities and Colleges Admissions Service. This is the central body for handling applications to universities. You can also search for courses on their website
WJEC	Welsh Joint Education Committee (Examining board for Wales)

Introduction

What next? This is a question that you will probably ask yourself at many points in your life, but it's a question that's especially important when you are thinking about your post-16 qualifications, education or occupations. Many of you will be considering doing further study after your GCSEs, and this book gives you details of the most popular options so you can make the most informed choice. The kinds of questions the book helps you answer include:

- What subjects are available?
- What are the most common post-16 options?
- How can I choose between different subjects?
- Which subjects do I need to go to university?
- How can I study effectively?
- What options are there if I want to take time out before Higher Education?

While the most popular post-16 study choice is GCE A/AS levels, you can also use this guide to find out about other types of qualifications including BTEC Nationals, Scottish Highers, the International Baccalaureate, the Welsh Baccalaureate, the new Advanced Diploma and many others. Furthermore, the book also tries to help answer broader questions that you may not have even considered asking yourself: do I actually want to do further study? Do I need to do further training? What are the best qualifications for certain jobs? Whatever your situation, it remains clear that getting the right answers to these questions is very important: snap decisions at this stage can have significant consequences later on in life. Hopefully, though, with the aid of this book, you will be able to navigate your way successfully through the qualifications maze and make the best choices for you. I wish you well in your journey.

How to use this book

You may already have realised from your experience of studying so far that everybody learns in a different way. In the same way, people read books differently. Some like to read them cover to cover; others prefer to start with the section that is most relevant to them. Indeed, you can approach this book in either way. For those of you of that need a complete introduction to A levels and their equivalents, I recommend reading through the book sequentially and making a note of any especially important points in a journal or notebook. For those of you that already have some knowledge but need help with a specific issue, then the following table should be able to point you to the most relevant areas:

	A level (or equivalent) issue	Which section of the book?
1	I want to do further study after my GCSEs (or equivalent), but I'm not sure whether A levels are the best option.	See 'What are the options?' in Part One, pages 3
2	I need to find out about the different kinds of post-16 qualifications.	See 'What are the options?' and 'Choosing your qualification' in Part One, pages 3 and 13
3	I can't decide on my third subject choice. How can I decide between two subjects I really enjoy?	See 'Choosing your subject', page 21
4	I know what I want to study at university but I'm not sure which A levels or equivalents I should choose.	See 'Choosing your subjects' in Part One, page 21; and Part Two
5	I want to improve my effectiveness at studying, revision and taking exams.	See 'Making a success of your studies' in Part Three, page 195
6	I want to find out details about each A/AS level subject, and the subject details of other qualifications.	See Part Two
7	I want to go straight into work after my post-16 qualifications.	See 'Choosing your qualification' in Part One, page 13; Part Two (non-graduate jobs' section for relevant subjects); and 'End note: What next?' in Part Three, page 201
8	I want to find out about A level equivalents such as Scottish Highers, IB and BTEC and apprenticeships.	See 'What are your options?' and 'Choosing your qualification' in Part One, pages 3 and 13
9	I want to find out which qualification is best for certain types of work or further study.	See 'Choosing your qualification' in Part One, page 13
10	I want some ideas about what to do after my post-16 qualification.	See 'End note: What next?'

PART ONE

OPTIONS AND DECISIONS

CHAPTER ONE

What are the options?

This chapter gives you an outline of the most popular post-16 qualification and training options

There is no doubt that the more education you have, the easier it is to get into certain aspects of work. For some people it is taken as read that after their GCSEs they will go on and do further study, but have you ever stopped to ask yourself (or your son/daughter if you are a parent) any of the following questions:

- Am I good at studying?
- Do I enjoy studying?
- Have my results been good enough to warrant further study?
- Do I need to study further for the kind of job I want to do?
- Do I understand the degree of difficulty and volume of work that may be associated with further study?

If you've answered no to one or more of these questions, then it's probably worth taking some time to weigh up all the options before going ahead. The most popular options, including A levels, are outlined below.

GCE A levels and AS levels

A levels are probably the most widely known post-16 qualification and still seen as the traditional gateway to Higher Education. In the past, A levels consisted of a two-year course with exams at the end. In September 2000, the 16–19 education system was changed to encourage more breadth of knowledge and learning among young people. Now, the A level consists of two parts: the AS and the A2.

The Advanced Subsidiary (AS) is a stand-alone qualification and is valued as half a full A level qualification. It has three units (assessed at the standard expected for a student half way through an A level course) that contribute 50 per cent of the full A level. The A2 is the second half of a full A level qualification. It has three units (assessed at the standard expected for a student at the end of a full A level course) that are worth 50 per cent of the full A level qualification. Most units are assessed by examination. Some are assessed by coursework. In most A levels, coursework accounts for 20 to 30 per cent of the marks.

The AS covers the less demanding material in an A level course. The A2 covers the more demanding material. For example, in the A2, students might:

- specialise in an area they studied at AS
- extend their knowledge and understanding of the subject by studying new topics
- improve their skills.

Also in the A2, students will combine knowledge, understanding and skills from across the A level course. AS levels and A levels are still probably the most traditionally academic qualifications for 16-19 year olds.

GCEs/A levels in Applied Subjects

These types of A levels replace VCE A levels. The new qualifications give students a broad introduction to a vocational area and may use different methods of assessment compared to traditional A levels such as case studies and work-related portfolios. The qualifications are available in both 'AS' and 'A' level, but, at the current time, only in the following 10 subject areas:

Applied Art and Design	Health and Social care
Applied Business	Leisure Studies
Applied ICT	Media: communication and production
Applied Science	Performing Arts
Engineering	Travel and Tourism

Key Skills

As the post-16 education sector has been changing, there has been a greater emphasis on developing skills as well as acquiring knowledge. So much so that Key Skills are now part of the new National Qualifications Framework (NQF). The most important skills that have been identified for everybody to have are:

1. **Communication:** Reading, writing, speaking and listening. These are not just important for courses in Modern Languages but for all subjects.

2. **Application of number:** Acquiring the ability to use numbers, graphs and data in a variety of contexts and for a variety of purposes. It's not just about doing calculations, but also about showing that you have numerical reasoning ability.

3. **Information Technology (IT):** Using hardware and software in different ways for different purposes. Most subjects now use IT or Computing to a greater or lesser extent as do the vast majority of jobs.

4. **Working with others:** This is about being an active and responsible team member and learning to relate to others in a group situation effectively.

5. **Improving one's own learning and performance:** This is about self-development and recognising strengths and weaknesses, a crucial aspect of personal and career development.

6. **Problem solving:** The ability to analyse situations and generate creative solutions to solve problems.

Three of the skills are available as a qualification – communication, application of number and information technology. Schools and colleges vary a lot in terms of whether they offer this option to students: some do, some don't. Equally, many Higher Education institutions, particularly most prestigious ones, may not accept this as counting towards your points tally for entry onto a degree course.

Advanced Extension Award

AEAs are designed to challenge the most able advanced level students, ensuring that they are tested against standards comparable with the most demanding found in other countries. They are designed to be accessible to all able students, whatever their school or college and whichever specification they are studying. They will also help universities differentiate between the most able candidates, particularly in subjects with a high proportion of A grades at advanced level.

The International Baccalaureate (IB)

This programme was set up to establish a common curriculum and university entry qualification for students moving from one country to another. It was thought that students should share an academic experience that would emphasise critical thinking, intercultural understanding and exposure to a variety of points of view. The programme has earned a reputation for rigorous assessment, giving IB Diploma holders access to the world's leading universities. The programme is a comprehensive two-year international curriculum available in English, French and Spanish.

Students study six subjects, and they have to choose one from each of the following subject groups:

- **Language 1** (students immerse themselves in the language, literature and culture of their native country)
- **Language 2** (students learn a second language)
- **Individuals and societies** (students choose an option from business and management, economics, geography, history, Islamic history, IT, philosophy, psychology and social and cultural anthropology)
- **Experimental Sciences** (options are biology, chemistry, physics, environmental sciences and design and technology)
- **Mathematics and Computer Science** (students have different types of mathematics course to choose. Computer science is optional)
- **The Arts** (options include visual arts, music and theatre arts).

Normally, three of the subjects are studied at higher level (HL) and the remaining three subjects are studied at standard level (SL). As well as the six compulsory subjects, there are three core components: the extended essay (4,000-word independent research); theory of knowledge (interdisciplinary study); and creativity, action, service (students are required to take part in artistic pursuits, sports and community service work). Each of the six modules are graded on a seven point scale, with seven representing the highest. The Theory of Knowledge and Extended Essay are worth a maximum of three points. Therefore students can achieve up to a maximum score of 45.

The IB is recognised widely both by universities and recruiters across the globe.

National Vocational Qualifications (NVQs)

NVQs are work-related, competence-based qualifications. They reflect the skills and knowledge needed to do a job effectively and show that a candidate is competent in the area of work the NVQ framework represents. NVQs are based on national occupational standards. These standards are statements of performance that describe what competent people in a particular occupation are expected to be able to do. NVQs are achieved through assessment and training. Assessment is normally through on-the-job observation and questioning. Candidates produce evidence to prove they have the competence to meet the NVQ standards. Assessors sign off units when the candidates are ready. The assessor tests candidates' knowledge, understanding and work-based performance to make sure they can demonstrate competence in the workplace.

There are five levels of NVQ:

- Level 1 = 5 GCSEs at grades D–G
- Level 2 = 5 GCSEs at grades A–C
- Level 3 = 2 A levels/1 vocational A level
- Level 4/5 = HNC, HND and degree level.

The New (Advanced) Diplomas

The Qualifications and Curriculum Authority (QCA) recently approved these qualifications and the Universities and Colleges Admissions Service (UCAS) has also made them part of the UCAS Tariff – the points system for entry into Higher Education.

There are various levels of Diploma, and the way they are graded will be aligned with GCSEs and A levels:

- **Foundation:** takes broadly the same time to do as four or five GCSEs, worth five grades D–G in GCSE terms
- **Higher:** takes broadly the same time to do as five or six GCSEs, worth seven grades A*–C
- **Advanced:** takes broadly the same time to do as three A levels, worth 3.5 A levels
- **Progression:** takes broadly the same time as two A levels and is aimed at those who cannot complete a whole Advanced Diploma.

The new Diplomas will come into place for the academic year 2008/9 and will initially be taught in construction and the built environment; information technology; creative and media, and society, health and development although, in time, the plan is to extend the Diploma for other subject areas.

The Diplomas are to be taught in a way that students experience a mixture of practical, theoretical and applied learning. You will learn about your particular subject area, but there is also a 'Functional Skills' element, which includes English, Mathematics and ICT. As well as this, there are some specialist options which students can take to complete the Diploma. The table below outlines the structure:

Principal learning	• Gives the industry title of the Diploma
	• Learning that is related to the sector of the economy
	• Learning that is designed and endorsed by industry
Core content	• Includes the assessment of Functional skills in English, ICT and Mathematics
	• Develops students' employability skills of teamwork and self-management
	• Gives the student the opportunity to produce and extended report
	• Requires at least 10 days' work experience
Additional and/or specialist learning	• Allows for students to specialise
	• Allows for the student to choose more qualifications
	• Allows for flexibility and choice of learning

In terms of the UCAS Tariff, the Advanced Diploma points are split with up to 300 for the 'principal learning' and 'core content' and 120 more for additional and specialist learning.

Students would be wise to do some careful research before opting for this route. The success of this qualification will depend on the extent to which universities and colleges embrace it. If you want to go to college or university after your post-16 study, then always check with their admissions officers to see whether the new Diplomas will be readily accepted for the particular subject you want to study.

For more information about the specific subject areas to be covered by the new Diplomas see the QCA website (www.qca.org.uk) and also check the websites of the relevant examination boards.

Modern Apprenticeships

Apprentices learn on the job, building up knowledge and skills, gaining qualifications and earning money all at the same time. There are different levels of apprenticeship available, but they all lead to NVQs Level 2 or 3 (see above), Key Skills qualifications and, in most cases, a technical certificate such as a BTEC or City & Guilds.

The kinds of subject potential apprentices can take include:

- Agriculture
- Administration
- Construction
- Customer service, retailing and wholesaling
- Engineering
- Finance, Insurance and Real Estate
- Health and Beauty
- Manufacturing
- Media and Printing
- Recreation and Travel
- Transportation.

You can opt to do an apprenticeship after your GCSEs but there are a number of things to consider. First, in order to do an apprenticeship, you need first to find an employer in that sector offering an opportunity. You may want to do an apprenticeship in Arts and Entertainment, for instance, but, if there are no employers offering apprenticeships in that field, you won't be able to do one. Secondly, the availability of apprenticeships varies according to the geographical area you may live in. Finally, whether or not you can do an apprenticeship also depends on your experience. Some employers want their apprentices to at least have had a bit of work experience in the relevant area first. Students under 19 can contact their local Connexions service for help with arranging work experience (www.connexions.org.uk). If you want to see a complete list of areas in which apprenticeships are available, then visit www.apprenticeships.org.uk.

If you are taking an apprenticeship after your GCSEs, then try and aim for one which will lead to, as part of the package of qualifications, an NVQ Level 3. It is also possible, in some cases, for students to use apprenticeships as a stepping stone to Higher Education but this depends largely on the subject of study. To find out for sure, you should check with the admissions department of the institutions concerned.

Apprenticeships are increasingly popular and are a good way to further your career plans, but they're not for everyone. Apprentices can receive good training but have to be committed to their job during the week. Reliability, being able to balance work and study and initiative are all important personal qualities shown by successful apprentices.

OCR Nationals

OCR Nationals are designed to cater for those who want to develop skills and knowledge through work-related learning. They provide candidates with high quality, industry-recognised certificates, geared to vocational sector requirements. Targeted primarily at post-16 learners, OCR Nationals will ultimately be available at Levels 1–3 of the National Qualifications Framework (see the following chapter). OCR Nationals can be delivered through flexible study programmes – either full time or part time, alongside other qualifications. Students can earn different amounts of UCAS points depending on the level studied and standard achieved.

BTEC (Business Technology and Education Council) Qualifications

The most appropriate BTEC qualification after GCSEs is BTEC Nationals. These qualifications are aimed to give students the practical skills in art and design needed by the job market in that particular sector. BTEC Nationals are available in three levels:

- BTEC National Award (equivalent to one GCE A level)
- BTEC National Certificate (equivalent to two GCE A levels)
- BTEC National Diploma (equivalent to three GCE A levels).

The BTEC Nationals can also be used to get into training or employment, but also Higher Education

The subjects available at BTEC National level are as follows:

Art and Design*	Business*	Construction
E-business	Engineering*	Hair and Beauty
Health and Care*	Hospitality and Catering	IT and Computing*
Land-based subjects	Logistics	Media, Music and Performing Arts*
Public Services	Retail	Science*
Sport*	Travel and Tourism*	

*These subjects have an entry in this guide. If you want to find out about a BTEC National subject not covered in this guide, then visit the Edexcel website: www.edexcel.org.uk.

Scottish Highers

The Scottish Higher qualification is taken in S5 and S6 (Year 12 and 13). It can lead to a job or entry to Further and Higher Education. Where A levels are taken over two years, it only takes one year to study for a Higher. Therefore it's common to take between four and six Highers in any one academic year. Like A levels, Highers have been revamped recently to improve the choice available to students. The new Highers provide a broader range of options for progression beyond the Scottish Standard Grade level. There are five levels:

- Access
- Intermediate 1
- Intermediate 2
- Higher
- Advanced Higher.

Having five levels means that there will be more scope to demonstrate your abilities at a level that's right for you. Each level is designed to encourage you to move on to the next.

Each qualification consists of three units, including an exam for all levels at Intermediate 1 and above. Each unit is a qualification in its own right (called National Units). There will be an exam in May/June on everything you have covered in the course, which will be combined with your coursework to give you a final grade. A full list of subjects that can be studied is on the Scottish Qualifications Authority website (www.sqa.org.uk), but here are the main ones:

Accounting and Finance	Drama	Physics
Administration	Economics	Politics
Applied Mathematics	Electronics	Product Design
Art & Design	Engineering	Psychology
Biology	French	Religious Studies
Biotechnology	Gaelic	Russian
Business Management	Geography	Science
Care	German	Sociology
Chemistry	History	Spanish
Classical Greek	Information Systems	Sport and Leisure
Classical Studies	Italian	Travel and Tourism
Communication & Media	Latin	Urdu
Computing	Maths	
Construction	Media Studies	
Contemporary Social Studies	Music	
Craft and Design	Philosophy	
Dance	Physical Education	

In theory, the Scottish Higher qualifications can be offered by schools or colleges throughout the world. In practice, they are mainly offered by schools and colleges in Scotland.

The Welsh Baccalaureate (WB)

The Welsh Baccalaureate (WB) provides a broad, diverse study curriculum for students aged 16–18 with a wider mix of subjects. Instead of taking three subjects, Welsh Baccalaureate Qualification (WBQ) students first study core subjects on contemporary Welsh life. Optional subjects can then be picked from courses already on offer through A levels and other qualifications. The emphasis is on work and industrial experience and the argument is that this will better prepare students for university or the workplace. The core has four elements (listed below) plus an individual investigation:

1.   Key Skills (see 'Key Skills' section on page 4 and 5).

2. Wales, Europe and the World (WEW). Students study how political, economic, social and cultural issues affect Wales, Europe and the World. This component also includes a language module.

3. Work-related Education (WRE). This option has two elements: 'Working with an Employer' and 'Taking part in a Team Enterprise activity.' The module improves their knowledge of the world of work and business as well as improving their knowledge of careers.

4. Personal and Social Education (PSE).

This module has five elements:

- An activity within the local community
- Citizenship
- Health
- Positive relationships
- Sustainable development.

As well as the core above, students complete their programme of study by choosing options including GCE A levels or NVQs. Before you decide on which options to choose within the WB, try and think what you want to do after the course. If you want to go to a particular Higher Education (HE) institution, always check with them that they will accept the particular Welsh Baccalaureate that you are following.

Post-GCSE students should be following the WB (Advanced Diploma). In terms of UCAS points, if you pass the core of the WB, you are credited with 120 points. This goes towards your total which is completed by the study of additional A levels or NVQs for example.

In theory, the WB qualification can be offered by schools or colleges throughout the world. In practice, they are mainly offered by schools and colleges in Wales.

The CACHE Diploma

CACHE stands for the Council for Awards in Childcare and Education. This is one of the main bodies that awards qualifications at different levels for those that want to specialise in working with children. The organisation offers Diplomas at different levels and attracts points on the UCAS Tariff, the system that calculates entry points for university.

Diploma in Foundation Studies

The primary aim of the Level 3 Diploma in Foundation Studies (Art & Design) is to educate students to make informed decisions which will help their progression to appropriate Higher Education in art and design. The Level 3 Diploma in Foundation Studies (Art & Design) builds on the students' prior experience and skills gained. The Level 3 Diploma in Foundation Studies in Art & Design comprises nine units, all of which are mandatory. These units are in three stages. There are three units in the first stage, four units in the second stage and two units in the final stage. This staged structure supports the progressive development of the student towards independent and self-reliant learning.

How to find out more each type of qualification

A levels and AS levels	see Part Two of this book
Advanced Diplomas	http://yp.direct.gov.uk/diplomas
International Baccalaureate	www.ibo.org
Modern Apprenticeships	www.apprenticeships.org.uk; www.scottishenterprise.com/ modernapprenticeships
NVQs	www.dfes.gov.uk/nvq
BTEC	www.edexcel.org.uk
OCR Nationals	www.ocr.org.uk; www.ucas.com
Scottish Highers	www.sqa.org.uk
The Welsh Baccalaureate	www.wbq.org.uk
The Cache Diploma	www.dfes.gov.uk; www.qca.org.uk
BTEC Diploma in Foundation Studies	www.edexcel.org.uk

So by now you should have an idea of some of the most common post-16 options, but how do you decide between them? The next chapter will show you how.

CHAPTER TWO

Choosing your qualification

In this section you will:

- *get help with choosing the right post-16 qualification*
- *learn about the UCAS Tariff*
- *find out how the different qualifications compare to one another in terms of academic level*
- *do a brief exercise to help you choose the right qualification.*

With so many different options it can be a bit overwhelming, so how do you go about making the best choice? One of the best ways of doing this is by comparing the qualifications with one another and by really focusing on what it is that you would like to do afterwards. Let's start by comparing the qualifications with one another.

One of the reasons why the government introduced something called the 'National Qualifications Framework' (NQF), is so that the various qualifications could be more easily compared. It's worth remembering that only qualifications recognised by the regulatory authorities are included in the NQF. The framework has recently been reviewed and an outline is given below (pay special attention to Level 3):

Qualification Level	What it means	Examples of qualifications or awards
Entry level	Involves learning basic knowledge and skills not geared towards specific occupations.	Qualifications are offered at Entry 1, 2 and 3 in a range of subjects
Level 1	Learning at this level is about activities that relate to everyday situations and possibly job competence	NVQ 1; Certificates in manual skills; GCSEs Grades D-G; OCR Nationals
Level 2	Learning at this level involves building knowledge and/or skills in relation to an area of work or a subject area and is appropriate for many job roles.	GCSEs Grades A*– C; NVQ 2; some certificates and Diplomas; apprenticeships; OCR Nationals

Level 3	Learning at this level involves obtaining detailed knowledge and skills. It is appropriate for people wishing to go to university, people working independently, or in some areas supervising and training others in their field of work.	A levels and AS levels; NVQ 3; Advanced Extension Awards (AEAs); A levels in Applied Subjects; BTEC National Diploma/Certificate/Award; Scottish Highers; IB; Welsh Baccalaureate; OCR Nationals
Level 4	Learning at this level is appropriate for people working in technical and professional jobs and/or managing and developing others. Level 4 qualifications are at a level equivalent to Certificates of Higher Education.	BTEC HND/HNC; NVQ 4; Qualifications in some non-graduate professional areas
Level 5	Learning at this level involves the demonstration of high levels of knowledge, a high level of work expertise in job roles and competence in managing and training others. Qualifications at this level are appropriate for people working as higher-grade technicians, professionals or managers.	NVQ 5; HE Diplomas; Foundation degrees
Level 6	Learning at this level involves the achievement of a high level of professional knowledge and is appropriate for people working as knowledge-based professionals or in professional management positions.	Bachelors Honours Degrees; Postgraduate Diplomas in some professional areas (e.g. Management, Counselling, etc.)
Level 7	Learning at this level involves the mastery of a complex and specialised area of knowledge and skills. This level is important for people who want to work in highly specialised or research-based areas of work.	Masters Degrees; some specialist postgraduate Diplomas or certificates
Level 8	Achievement at this level involves making a significant and original contribution to a specialised field of enquiry. It is appropriate for people at the forefront of a field of work or research and who want to be pioneers.	Doctorates; specialist awards

In all probability, you will be choosing something from Level 3, but it is useful to see the other levels so you can compare what and how you will be studying. Level 3 qualifications are, in the vast majority of cases, the gateway to Higher Education (HE) and certain jobs.

The UCAS Tariff

Another way of comparing qualifications is to look at the UCAS Tariff of each one. The UCAS Tariff is a points system used to report achievement for entry to HE in a numerical format. In other words, institutions usually require a certain number of points to allow you to study there. Many employers also have a points threshold when selecting candidates. It establishes agreed equivalences between different types of qualifications and provides comparisons between applicants with different types and volumes of achievement. Points can be aggregated from the different qualifications included in the Tariff but there is no ceiling to the number of points which can be accumulated. Equally there is no double counting – applicants cannot count the same or similar qualifications twice. Achievement at a lower level will be subsumed into the higher level, i.e. AS points will be subsumed into the A level points for the same subject. The same principle applies to Scottish Highers and Advanced Highers and so on.

Below is a table setting out how the UCAS Tariff works in practice for the various different qualifications.

The following tables have been reproduced with the kind permission of UCAS.

| GCE/VCE Qualifications | | | | BTEC Nationals[1] | | | OCR Nationals[2] | | | Points | Advanced[3] Diploma | | Scottish Qualifications | | | | Irish Leaving Certificate | |
GCE AS/AS VCE	GCE AS Double Award	GCE A level/AVCE	GCE/AVCE Double Award	Award	Certificate	Diploma	Certificate	Diploma	Extended Diploma	Points	Diploma	ASL[4]	Advanced Higher	Higher	Int 2	Standard Grade	Higher	Ordinary
						DDD			D1	360								
						DDM			D2/M1	320								
										300	A							
						DMM			M2	280								
										250	B							
			AA		DD	MMM		D	M3	240								
			AB							220								
			BB		DM	MMP		M1	P1	200	C							
			BC							180								
			CC		MM	MPP		M2/P1	P2	160								
										150	D							
			CD							140								
	AA	A		D	MP	PPP	D	P2	P3	120		Max	A					
	AB									110								
	BB	B	DE							100	E		B					
	BC						M	P3		90							A1	
	CC	C	EE	M	PP					80			C					
										77							A2	
										72			D	A				
										71							B1	
	CD									70								
										64							B2	
A	DD	D								60				B				
										58							B3	
										52							C1	
B	DE									50								
										48				C				
										45							C2	
										42				D	A			
C	EE	E		P						40								
										39							C3	A1
										38						Band 1		
										35					B			
										33							D1	
D										30								
										28					C	Band 2		
										26							D2	A2
E										20							D3	B1
										14								B2
										7								B3

1 The points shown are for the BTEC National Award, Certificate and Diploma introduced into centres from September 2002

2 Further information on OCR grades and Tariff points can be found on the UCAS website

3 The points for Advanced Diplomas come into effect for entry to Higher Education from 2010 onwards

4 Additional and Specialist Learning (ASL) can contribute a maximum of 120 points to the overall Tariff score for the Advanced Diploma

BTEC Nationals in Early Years (Theory)		CACHE Diploma in Child Care & Education			Points	Diploma in Foundation Studies (Art and Design)	Diploma in Fashion Retail	iPRO		AAT NVQ Level 3 in accounting[5]
Certificate	Diploma	Practical	Theory	Practical	Points			Certificate	Diploma	
	DDD				320					
					285	D				
	DDM				280					
	DMM				240					
			AA		225	M				
	MMM				220					
DD			BB		200					
					165	P				
DM	MMP		CC		160		D			P
MM	MPP		DD	A	120		M			
				B	100				Pass	
MP	PPP		EE	C	80		P	Pass		
				D	60					
PP				E	40					

[5] Points for the AAT Level 3 NVQ in Accounting come into effect for entry to Higher Education in 2009 onwards

British Horse Society			Points	Music Examinations[6]						Speech and Drama Examinations[7]			
Stage 3 Horse Knowledge & Care	Stage 3 Riding	Preliminary Teacher's Certificate		Practical Grade 6	Practical Grade 7	Practical Grade 8	Theory Grade 6	Theory Grade 7	Theory Grade 8	Grade 6	Grade 7	Grade 8	PCertLAM[8]
			90										D
			80										M
			75			D							
			70			M							
			65									D	
			60		D							M	P
			55		M	P					D		
			50								M		
			45	D								P	
			40	M	P					D	P		
		Pass	35							M			
	Pass		30						D				
			25	P					M				
			20					D	P	P			
Pass			15					M					
			10					P					
			5				P						

6 Points shown are for ABRSM,Guildhall,LCMM,Rockschool and Trinity College London advanced level music examinations

7 Points shown are for LAMDA,LCMM and Trinity Guildhall advanced level speech and drama examinations accredited by the National Qualifications Framework and come into effect for entry to Higher Education in 2008 onwards. A full list of the subjects covered can be found on the UCAS website

8 Points for the LAMDA Level 3 Certificate in Speech and Drama: Performance Studies (PCertLAM) come into effect for entry to Higher Education in 2009 onwards

International Baccalaureate[9]	Points
Diploma	
45	768
44	744
43	722
42	698
41	675
40	652
39	628
38	605
37	582
36	559
35	535
34	512
33	489
32	466
31	442
30	419
29	396
28	373
27	350
26	326
25	303
24	280

Free-standing Maths[10]	IFS CeFS[11]	IFS DipFS[12]	COPE[13]	Advanced Extension Awards[14]	Points	Core Skills	Key Skills	Welsh Baccalaureate Core[15]
					120			Pass
					70			
	A	A	Pass		60			
	B	B			50			
	C	C		D	40			
	D	D			30		Level 4	
A	E	E		M	20	Higher	Level 3	
B					17			
C					13			
D					10	Int 2	Level 2	
E					7			

10 Covers free-standing Mathematics qualifications – Additional Maths, Using and Applying Statistics, Working with Algebraic and Graphical Techniques, Modelling with Calculus
11 Points shown are for the revised Institute of Financial Services Certificate in Financial Studies (CeFS) taught from September 2003
12 Points shown are for the Institute of Financial Services Diploma in Financial Studies (DipFS) and come into effect for entry to Higher Education in 2008
13 Points are awarded for the Certificate of Personal Effectiveness (COPE) awarded by ASDAN and CCEA
14 Points for Advanced Extension Awards are over and above those gained from the A level grade
15 Points for the Core are awarded only when a candidate achieves the Welsh Baccalaureate Advanced Diploma

9 The points for the International Baccalaureate are awarded to candidates who achieve the IB Diploma

EDI Level 3 Certificates in Accounting and Accounting (IAS)[16]	Points	Higher Sports Leader Award[17]	Advanced Placement Programme[18]		Extended Project[19]
			Group A	Group B	
Distinction	120		5		
Credit	90		4		
Pass	70				
	60		3		A
	50			5	B
	40				C
	35			4	
	30	Pass			D
	20			3	E

[16] The points for the Education Development International (EDI) Level 3 Certificates in Accounting and Accounting (IAS) come into effect for entry to Higher Education from 2009 onwards

[17] The points for the Higher Sports Leader Award come into effect for entry to Higher Education from 2009 onwards

[18] Details of the subjects covered by each group can be found on the UCAS websiteof the subjects covered by each group can be found on the UCAS website

[19] The points for the Extended Project come into effect for entry to Higher Education from 2010 onwards

The next section focuses on choosing between specific subjects, mainly with A levels in mind. If you need more specific subject information on other Level 3 qualifications, look at the relevant websites listed at the end of Chapter 1.

CHAPTER THREE

Choosing between A levels and equivalent subjects

This chapter includes:

- *answers to the most common questions by prospective students*
- *exercises to help you decide between subjects*
- *a breakdown of the A level results from summer 2004*
- *sources of further information.*

It seems sensible to dedicate a section on the kinds of things to consider when you're trying to choose between different subjects as this is one of the dilemmas that students face when thinking about their options. Some of the following questions tend to be the most frequently asked:

Should I choose those subjects I am strongest in?

This is a good a reason as any to choose a subject at Advanced level. Think about the subjects you've studied so far at GCSE and which ones you've had the best results in. This should give you the confidence that you could study it at a higher level. There is quite a jump in difficulty between GCSE and Level 3 qualifications.

Should I choose those subjects I enjoy the most?

It's possible that you can be good at a subject and not enjoy it, and vice versa. However, experience shows that those who go for subjects they are really interested in tend to do better. This is largely because they have a natural talent for that area but also because they are likely to have the motivation to do the reading around the subject needed to get the top grades. One word of warning though: if you go for subject that you enjoy, check which HE courses you are ruling out by making this choice.

If you are struggling to think about what your natural talents are, the following table might help you. Look at the skills on the left-hand side of the table and think which ones you'd definitely like to use in further study, and those which you definitely wouldn't like to use. Put a tick or a cross in each case. Then look to see which subjects match which skills, and see if that sheds any light on where your natural talents lie.

Name of skill	I like this using this skill	I hate using this skill	Subjects that require this skill a lot
Communication skills (good at communicating, reading, writing essays, learning languages)			All subjects, but especially arts; humanities and social science subjects such as English; History; Sociology and Modern Languages; Media and Communication
Attention to detail (being good with small details, checking facts, figures, specifics, quantities)			All science subjects, as well as Geography; History; Engineering; Archaeology and IT; Geology
Physical ability (e.g. making things, doing things, exercising, using your hands, doing experiments)			Physical Education; Engineering; Archaeology and IT; Photograph; Art & Design and Design & Technology
Creative ability (e.g. making things, writing or drawing, performing)			Art & Design; Design & Technology; English Literature; Drama; Performing Arts; Music
Memory and recall skills (memorising facts, words, vocabulary and theories)			Many subjects, but especially History; Maths; Sciences; Philosophy; Modern Languages; Latin/Greek.
IT and computing skills (using hardware, software and systems)			IT/Computing; Archaeology; Design & Technology; Music Technology; Engineering; Physics; Technology; Geology
Mathematical skills (using figures and stats to conclude and investigate things; doing mental calculations).			Maths; all Sciences, especially Physics; Engineering; Psychology; Design & Technology; Geography; Geology
Emotional Intelligence skills (empathising; intuition; vision; creativity; tact; interpersonal skills)			Religious Studies; English Literature; History of Art; Communication Studies; Psychology; History; Classical Civilisation; Music
Spatial awareness and mechanical skills (being able to 'see' what shapes will fit where; making and working with mechanical objects)			Engineering; Physics; Art & Design; Design & Technology; Computing/IT; Construction and the Built Environment
Business skills (understanding business, finance and economics, as well as specific sectors of work)			Accounting; Business Studies; Economics; Law; Travel and Tourism; Retail and Distributive Services; Leisure and Recreation

Citizenship skills (being familiar with and learning about social, political and environmental issues of the past and present)	Ancient History; Classical Civilisation; Geography; History; Environmental Science; Politics and Government; Law; Philosophy; Latin/Greek; Sociology; Social Policy; Religious Studies; English Literature; Media Studies

How are the different subjects assessed?

Most A levels, AS levels and equivalents such as Scottish Highers, are assessed by a combination of written exams (either at the end or during your course), coursework (essays, projects or case studies) completed during the course in your own time, and practical exams (especially for Science subjects or others where certain practical skills are needed). Not only is there variation between subjects in terms of the type of assessment, but there also will be some variation among different examination boards offering the same subject. So try and work out whether you are better at exams or coursework or practical work and bear that in mind when choosing your particular subjects.

Which subjects are best to get into Higher Education?

That very much depends on what you want to study. If you know you want to study a particular subject at university already, then in most cases it's expected that you have an A level or equivalent with a good grade in that subject. However, there are some subjects where it's not clear which subject areas are required because that subject isn't widely offered (if at all) at Level 3. Also, some degree subjects specify more than one particular A level or equivalent.

Should I choose subjects that are similar to one another?

That partly depends on the kind of person you are. Some people like to specialise (and for example take all science or arts subjects), others prefer to have a taste of both. It doesn't really matter so long as you realise what the UCAS requirements for your Higher Education course or grades needed for the kind of job you're interested in. Ensure, however, that there is not too much overlap between subjects otherwise it might detrimentally affect your UCAS points total.

Do I need a GSCE in a subject to do it at GCE A/AS level?

Not necessarily. If you can convince your tutors or teachers that you have the right academic potential as well as the right attitude then it is possible in some cases. However, there are subjects that really build on the knowledge you've learned at GCSE. These include:

• Languages
• Maths
• Sciences.

It would be rather difficult to pick these subjects up at Advanced level without any of the building blocks. There are, however, subjects that are not studied at GCSE level that most people meet for the first time at A level and assume no prior knowledge. These include, among others:

- Business
- Government and Politics
- Law
- Philosophy
- Sociology

. . . as well as a number of others.

Is it true that it's easier to get good grades in some subjects compared with others?

In general, students do best at the subjects they're most interested in and what they enjoy. If you want to see the breakdown of A/AS level results from previous years, visit www.jcgq.org.uk.

How can I find out more?

If you need further information at this point, it's worth remembering the following sources of information can be very useful:

- Tutors
- UCAS – the central admissions organisation for entry into HE (visit www.ucas.com)
- The admissions departments of universities you're interested in applying to Connexions Services, who give advice and guidance for young people: www.connexions.gov.uk.

By now you should have lots of information about what to consider when choosing A level or equivalent subjects. Once you've come up with a shortlist, go the next chapter to look at the relevant subject areas in detail. This should hopefully confirm your choice or it may make you reconsider. Either way, it's essential information before you make your final decision.

PART TWO

DIRECTORY OF SUBJECTS

How to use the directory

The following directory has lots of information about subjects you can study after GCSEs (or equivalent). In practice, this often means GCE A levels and AS levels but, where relevant, each subject includes other possible qualifications such as BTEC qualifications, Advanced Extension Awards (AEAs), NVQs and other qualifications. Please bear in mind, however, that it does not include every single subject that it's possible to study, but it does outline the vast majority on offer. Much of the information will also apply to Scottish Higher subjects as well as other types of qualification but for the exact details of courses and assessment methods, always check with your school, college or exam board.

Each section has includes the following: a description of the subject; the qualifications available and a brief outline of the course structure and assessment methods the main elements of the exam board specifications; future career options, including further study and employment. As you browse the directory, try to have in mind the following questions:

- Would I enjoy studying this?
- Would I do well in the subject, given the type of assessment methods used?
- How would choosing this subject affect my further study options?
- How would choosing this subject affect my employment options?

Then come up with a shortlist of subjects and if you are still finding it difficult to choose between a few subjects, revisit Chapter 3 in Part One of this book.

ACCOUNTING

Good financial information is a key requirement for success in most areas of life. It is essential for businesses, for governments, for households and for individuals. Traditionally, accountants had to do two things: provide a record of trading activity and act as independent auditors of the activity. Accountants learn this but they also deal with issues such as tax liabilities, act as company directors, or work with senior managers in business to help them plan their commercial activities.

Accounting is mainly divided into two areas: financial accounting and management accounting. The former deals with checking a company's accounts and preparing the annual accounts; management accountants usually work for a particular company and assist managers with budgeting and financial planning.

Subject options

For people without prior practical experience, this subject is available in A and AS level. The subject is also available as a Vocationally Related Qualification (VRQ), as an NVQ but both of these qualifications are for people who already working in accounting (see section on non-graduate jobs).

A/AS level

Students of A level accounting will learn much of this and therefore they will need a keen interest in business, good attention to detail and a sound head for figures. If you've struggled at GCSE Maths, this may not be the subject for you. The outline below is based on what the majority of A level exam board syllabuses include, but based broadly on the OCR syllabus. For an exact definition of the AS and A2 syllabus you will be studying, you should consult your school or college or even the exam board itself.

Principles of accounting (AS)
An introduction to accounting; accounting concepts; expenditure classifications; ledge entries and adjustments; final accounts.

Applying accounting (AS)
The Journal; correction of errors; control accounts; adjustments; ICT in accounting; an introduction to budgeting.

Company accounts and interpretation (A2)
Preparation of final accounts for limited companies; financing; accounting standards; analysis and interpretation of accounts.

Management accounting (A2)
Budgets and budgetary control; financing; standard costing and variance analysis; capital expenditure appraisal; stock; costing; social responsibility.

How is A/AS level Accounting taught and assessed?

In the first instance, students will be introduced to the principles of accounting and then, over time, students will start to apply the principles to real situations. Therefore, the experience of studying this subject will be a mixture of learning theories and applying principles to business case studies. Assessment is by examination.

Choosing other subjects to go with Accounting

Popular choices include Business Studies, Computing, Law, Economics, Mathematics and some Science subjects. If you want to study Accounting at degree level, be aware that some universities require A level Mathematics. For other degree subjects (mainly arts and humanities) at some universities A level Accounting is not recognised as an entry qualification. If you already know what and where you want to study at a higher level, always check with the institution before finally choosing your subject.

Accounting at HE level

Given that Accounting is still not as established an A level as some other subjects, most universities do not require A level Accounting as an entry pre-requisite for their degree course. In fact, some prefer more 'traditional' A levels as opposed to Accounting or Business Studies. Most usually require a good grade at A level Mathematics however. Many degree courses are called Accounting and Finance rather than just Accounting and some include some elements of Economics and Computing.

A degree in Accounting?

At degree level, Accounting usually covers some core modules in both the first and second years and there are usually some further options that students can choose in their final year. One thing to consider when choosing your HE course is whether or not it gives you the opportunity to gain exemption from professional accountancy examinations. Some courses do, some don't.

Combining Accounting with other degree subjects

Accounting can be combined with almost any other subject of choice but popular ones include Economics, Computing, Business Management, Law, Finance, Mathematics and many others. However, as mentioned above, be careful when you combine with other subjects: it may affect your exemptions from professional examinations later on.

Accounting and your future career

Non-graduate jobs

It is possible to become a qualified accountant without going to university. You would have to complete a four-year training contract with a firm of accountants and take the necessary professional studies and examinations. You will need good grades at A level (at least 3 Cs) and the aptitude and temperament to successfully complete substantial further study. You could also consider working for an accounts department of any organisation as an accounts assistant or an accounts technician. Once you are working in accountancy, you could also consider work-based qualifications such as an NVQ Level 2 or 3 in Accounting or a Vocationally-Related Qualification (VRQ). These are offered by some of the main examination boards.

You would, of course, be able to go for any other jobs that are open to non-graduates. Those that require numerical skills, attention to detail and an interest in business would be suitable for those having done A level Accounting.

Graduate jobs directly related to Accounting (and Finance)

To obtain a professional accountancy qualification, you will need to follow your degree with further study leading to professional examinations, together with a period of approved work experience.

Various types of accountancy: you could be employed by a firm of accountants providing financial or business advice and other management services to a wide range of fee paying clients from the private individual to large commercial organisations and government bodies. Or you could be employed by a blue-chip organisation or public sector organisation and work with departmental managers to help them understand financial information. There are also many other different accountancy roles open to you.

Graduate jobs where Accounting (and Finance) could be useful

The knowledge and skills gained in this degree subject would be relevant to jobs across the financial and business sector. Some examples of these work areas follow.

- **Corporate, commercial and investment banking:** there is a wide range of generalist and specialist jobs in this area. Corporate financiers tasks include advising clients on the raising of capital whereas operations professionals ensure the transactions run smoothly.
- **Financial management:** important in all sectors of business, industry and commerce. There are opportunities to work in the public sector, e.g. NHS Financial Management. Large companies may employ corporate treasurers.
- **Insurance and pensions and actuarial work:** jobs in insurance include managing pension funds and the underwriting of insurance claims.
- **Investment management:** traders and stockbrokers are employed by banks. Not a career choice for the shy and timid!
- **Management consultancy:** Management consultants are called in to help solve organisational problems that a company might have. This could be in almost area including finances, IT, human resources and so on. It is a competitive area to get into.

- **Retail banking and personal financial services:** bank managers may manage several branches with responsibility for meeting sales targets and attracting new business. Credit analysts undertake risk assessments on loan requests.
- **Taxation:** either as a tax adviser, providing advisory and consultancy services in order to create the best tax strategies for your clients, or as a tax inspector determining tax liability on behalf of the Inland Revenue.

Further information

AccountingWeb	www.accountingweb.co.uk
The Association of Chartered Certified Accountants (ACCA)	www.acca.co.uk
Chartered Institute of Management Accountants	www.cimaglobal.com
Chartered Institute for Public Finance and Accountancy (CIPFA)	www.cipfa.org.uk
The Institute of Chartered Accountants in England and Wales (ICAEW)	www.icaew.co.uk

ARCHAEOLOGY

Archaeology literally means the study of things ancient. In particular, it's about understanding history from studying relics and antiquities that have been excavated from the land beneath our feet. This subject draws on other disciplines such as information technology, science, literature, but its closest ally is History. In the absence of any written records, Archaeology is often the only other means of identifying key events and civilisations of the past. Students of A level Archaeology learn, among other things, how sites are identified for excavation, how to interpret and date the findings, how settlements are formed and many other things.

Subject options

This subject is available in GCE A level and AS level.

A/AS level

The outline below is based on what the majority of A level exam board syllabuses include. For an exact definition of the AS and A2 syllabus you will be studying, you should consult your school or college or even the exam board itself. Students for the AS award will study 50 per cent of the modules that are needed for the A2 award.

Survey and excavation

In this module students learn about: how and why sites are excavated; how to carry out field work, using aerial photographs, understanding the environment and working with the community, detecting objects in the earth (using techniques such as metal detection); techniques for carrying out surveys.

Post-excavation, dating and interpretation (techniques and methods)

In this aspect of the course, students learn how to analyse the material they have recorded from a survey or excavation; typology; environmental analysis including pollen dating; general principles of chemical and physical analysis; how to date and interpret recorded material using a variety of techniques.

Religion and ritual

This module is about archaeological information and what it tells us about religion and ritual from various cultures. Schools can choose to apply this in a variety of contexts including pre-historic Britain and Ireland; ancient Egypt; The Mayan age; The Roman World to AD476.

Settlement and social organisation

This aspect of the course introduces students to the various different types of settlements that archaeologists study and excavate including domestic, agricultural, public or religious settlements. Social organisation teaches students how they could realistically assume what a particular society was like using the archaeological evidence.

Material culture and technology

This module of the course introduces the study of art and artefacts as well as the study of how societies in the past grew food and exploited the animal and vegetable resources for survival but also for trade and they transported those resources.

Personal study

Students may also have to submit a personal study based on fieldwork or personal research that is approved by the exam board.

How is A/As level Archaeology taught and assessed?

Like many subjects, there will be much classroom work and reading from textbooks. But Archaeology is different in that it often involves visits to sites of archaeological interests where students can see for themselves the relevance of their subject. As mentioned above, students often have to complete a personal study which can account for 20 per cent of their final marks. The other marks are given according to performance in written exams.

Choosing other subjects to go with Archaeology

Other subjects which go well with Archaeology are History; Geography; Art; Languages; Classical Civilisation; Latin and Classical Greek. But as with all subjects, there is no reason why students can't combine this with science-related or mathematically based subjects.

Archaeology at HE level

Archaeology is a well-established subject at HE level, even though it still remains a fairly specialised area. Students from this course gain both practical and analytical skills so they have a lot to offer employers. You may not need an A level (or equivalent) in Archaeology to study it at HE level but some institutions could want you to have an A level in History, Ancient History or Classical Civilisation.

A degree in Archaeology?

Archaeology degrees can vary quite a lot. Some are relatively 'modern' in their application of the practical skills of archaeology; others focus more on classical archaeology and its relationship with classical culture such as the arts, religion and literature. You have to decide what kind of archaeology you're most interested in. All courses will have elements of fieldwork which students usually carry out during the Easter and summer holidays.

Combining Archaeology with other degree subjects

Archaeology figures quite highly in joint degrees where you can concentrate on two allied disciplines. Common choices include:

- Archaeology and Ethnography
- Architectural History and Archaeology

- Archaeology and Social Anthropology
- Classics and Archaeology
- Geography and Archaeology.

Foundation degrees and Diplomas

There are a few BTEC Higher Nationals and Foundation degrees in Archaeology and related areas. These are useful for students who want to learn the vocational skills in the area rather than purely from an academic viewpoint.

Archaeology and your future career

Non-graduate jobs

The study of archaeology gives students a useful mix of both practical and intellectual skills. The skills of analysis, evaluation, IT ability, weighing up evidence and making reasoned judgements are all useful skills in any job. There may be some assistant or clerical level work you can start off in museums or galleries that also may require some of your archaeological skills and knowledge. Furthermore, some administrative positions, particularly in the Civil Service, demand the kinds of qualities mentioned above.

Graduate jobs directly related to Archaeology

Archaeologists can also be found in national heritage agencies; local authorities; national parks; nationally and local government funded museums; universities and colleges; archaeological societies; consultancies; and independent museums, trusts and charities. The main vocational areas related to this subject are:

- **Archaeologist:** working with, or leading, a team to plan and excavate, analyse finds and complete reports of findings.
- **HE lecturer:** teach Archaeology and carry out research activities in universities and some colleges of Further Education.

Graduate jobs where a degree in Archaeology could be useful

- **Heritage manager:** conserves, interprets and promotes historic buildings and sites. Manages facilities at the site. Organises exhibitions and events, developing displays on the historic interest of the site.
- **Historic buildings inspector/conservation officer:** inspects and reports on buildings of special historic or architectural interest for purpose of preservation or long-term conservation.
- **Museum/art gallery curator:** responsible for care and improvement of a collection including exhibitions, catalogues and organisation.
- **Museum education officer:** creates a link between a museum collection (or a number of museums) and the interests or needs of visitors. They are responsible for developing learning opportunities, which can be either informal or curriculum based.

- **Museum/gallery exhibitions officer:** responsible for activities and tasks associated with the planning and organising of permanent and travelling exhibitions. A pre-entry postgraduate qualification, such as an MA/Diploma in Museum Studies, is highly desirable.
- **Tourism officer:** promotes heritage as an attraction to incoming tourists including marketing and promoting facilities, information provision and development of facilities.

Careers open to all graduates

It is estimated that about 60 per cent of graduate jobs are open to students irrespective of their degree subject. What tends to interest employers most are previous experience as well as skills, potential and personal qualities. It's important to get involved in outside activities while you're a student so that the whole range of employers will be interested in your portfolio of skills and abilities.

Further information

The Council for British Archaeology   www.britarch.ac.uk

Current Archaeology   www.archaeology.co.uk

English Heritage   www.english-heritage.org.uk

ART AND DESIGN (APPLIED)

The courses available in Art and Design give students a practical and theoretical understanding of art and design in a variety of contexts. It equips them with the skills to continue further study, training or move into employment within the art and design field. Students learn a range of creative techniques – at one end of the spectrum this could be a painting or drawing methods, at the other end it could be how to create a 'practical' design for a new living space. One thing most art and design students have in common is a visual appreciation of their environment and they will learn different ways of conveying that vision through different media including decorative arts; sculpture; graphic design; ceramics; textiles and photography. From a theoretical point of view, students may also consider how art forms have developed over time and how they relate to their literary, social and political contexts.

Subject options

There are three main post-16 qualifications in Art and Design: GCE A/AS level in Applied Art and Design; BTEC Diploma in Foundation Studies (Art and Design); and BTEC Nationals in Art and Design.

A/AS level

The outline below is based on what the AQA exam board offers. For an exact definition of the AS and A2 syllabus you will be studying, you should consult your school or college or even the exam board itself.

Investigation of 2D visual language	Investigation of 3D visual language
Working to a brief	Historical and contemporary contexts
Professional Practice, communication and meaning	Application and development of 2D visual language
Application and development of 3D visual language	Working to self-identified briefs
Cultural and critical studies	Drawing, painting or sculpture and printmaking
Photography and lens-based imagery	Graphic design
Art in the community	Textile art and fashion
3D design	

If possible, students should have studied Art (or Art and Design) at GCSE level or have taken a BTEC First Diploma in Art and Design, but this is not always required by schools and colleges. Although there may be some theoretical elements to the course, in essence art and design is a very practical and vocationally based course. Students will be doing a lot of independent work in the art room or studio under the guidance of their teacher. Assessment is through a combination of producing portfolios of work and examinations. *(NB: Students should also be aware that GCE A/AS levels are also available in: Graphic Design; Textiles; and Three Dimensional Design.)*

BTEC Diploma in Foundation Studies (Art and Design)

The aim of this course is to prepare students for the different pathways into art and design, primarily in terms of Higher Education. The course consists of three distinct stages: the exploratory stage, the pathway stage and the confirmatory stage and each has specific units attached (see the table below):

The Exploratory stage	The Pathway stage	The Confirmatory stage
Encourages students to explore their interests, skills and creativity in art and design	*Examines more closely specialisms within the subject such as art, craft and design. Helps develop students' portfolios, CVs and presentation skills*	*Comprises two units that make up the externally assessed final project*
Unit 1: Information and Research in Art and Design	Unit 4: Information and Interpretation in Art and Design	Unit 7: Preparation and Progression in Art and Design
Unit 2: Recording and Responding in Art and Design	Unit 5: Personal Experimental Studies in Art and Design	Unit 8: Integrating Theory and Practice in Art and Design
Unit 3: Media Experimentation in Art and Design	Unit 6: Extended Media Development in Art and Design	Unit 9: Personal Confirmatory Study in Art and Design

This course is offered and assessed by the Edexcel exam board. For further details of each unit, visit their website. Units one to seven must be passed before moving on the final two 'confirmatory' units are begun. Assessment of the units is by portfolio of evidence. The final major project units (eight and nine) are assessed and graded together for the final award which will be Pass, Merit or Distinction.

BTEC Nationals

These qualifications are aimed to give students the practical skills in art and design needed by the job market in that particular sector. BTEC Nationals are available in three levels – Award, Certificate and Diploma.

Each of the following Art and Design related subjects can be studied at any one of the above levels:

- Art and Design
- Art and Design (3D Design)

- Art and Design (Design and Crafts)
- Art and Design (Fashion and Clothing)
- Art and Design (Fine Art)
- Art and Design (Graphic Design)
- Art and Design (Interactive Media)
- Art and Design (Photography)
- Art and Design (Textiles).

As an example of the content of the courses, the BTEC National Award in Art and Design is structured in the following way. Students must complete four core courses: Visual Recording in Art and Design; Materials, Techniques and Processes in Art and Design; Ideas and Concepts in Art and Design; and Visual Communication in Art and Design. Students then choose two specialist options to complete the course requirements. For Certificate and Diploma level, students complete five core courses and need to take extra specialist options to complete the qualification. Assessment is by a combination of coursework, projects, case studies and examinations.

Choosing other subjects to go with Art and Design

Most specialist courses at Higher Education would require post-16 qualification in Art and Design as well as least one other subject. Your choice of supporting subjects really depends on the kind of course you want to do after, if any. If you're interested in architecture, for instance, you may need qualifications in Maths and IT to help your applications; if you're interested in theatre design choosing English Literature and Drama could help your cause. If, on the other hand, you want to work as an artist after your post-16 qualifications, then choosing business or accounting may also help your chances of long-term success.

A degree in Art and Design?

Degree courses tend to specialise a bit more than any previous study and may split the whole field of art and design into specific degree programmes. The following are typical examples:

- BA (Hons) Design
- BA (Hons) Fashion Studies
- BA (Hons) Fine Art
- BA (Hons) Textiles.

Combining Art and Design with other degree subjects

Sometimes specific types of art and design degree programmes (such as the ones mentioned above) are combined together but other popular combining subjects include History of Art, Computing, Business Studies and Literature.

Art and Design and your future career

Non-graduate jobs

It's possible to get into some art and design-related jobs after A levels, such as working for a junior design assistant in a creative design agency. Other work that's possible to get experience in at this stage includes working as a marketing assistant and helping with the creative side of publications and promotions. Working as an assistant to a professional artist, photographer, designer or sculptor is also an option.

Graduate jobs directly related to Art and Design

Within art and design-related jobs, it is possible and quite common for a graduate to cross over to another discipline different from the one they studied, for example, fine art to graphic design. Related jobs include:

- **Arts administrator:** supports and generates artistic activity. The role may include marketing, promotion, book-keeping, finance and general administration. Appeals to those who want to combine working with art and people. Requires business and administration skills rather than creativity.
- **Exhibition/display designer:** organises the design of exhibition and display stands. Liaises with clients to produce designs that communicate their desired messages.
- **Fashion clothing designer:** produces designs for clothing and accessories. May specialise in an area such as sportswear.
- **Graphic designer:** produces visual solutions for the communication needs of clients. Needs creativity and imagination, good IT skills and commercial awareness.
- **Illustrator:** produces illustrations for magazines, books, advertising, brochures, greetings cards, packaging, posters or newspapers. Specialisms include scientific, technical and medical illustrators.
- **Museum/gallery conservator/restorer:** preserves and cares for collections of artistic or cultural objects. Many specialise in one type of object, for example furniture. Good class of degree and some voluntary experience often necessary for entry.
- **Textile designer:** creates designs in knit, weave or print to be used in the production of fabric or textile products.

Graduate jobs where a degree in Art and Design could be useful

- **Advertising art director:** creates visual ideas to be used within advertising. Works as part of a team alongside illustrators, photographers and those responsible for editorial. Can involve any media.
- **Art therapist:** works with people who present a variety of problems ranging from mental/physical illness, emotional and learning difficulties, stress and trauma. Aims to enable the client to effect change and growth on a personal level, within a safe environment, through the use of art materials.

- **Museum/art gallery curator:** acquires, cares for, stores and presents a collection of artefacts or works of art in order to inform, educate and entertain the public. May include other elements such as public relations, fund raising and customer care.
- **Picture researcher/editor:** finds suitable images for print and electronic publications. Investigates copyright, negotiates fees, liaises with clients. Part-time and distance learning courses are available.
- **Secondary school teacher:** appeals to those who are interested in developing the skills and knowledge of others within the art and design curriculum. Secondary school teaching mostly involves teaching art or design, craft, or technology as part of the National Curriculum.
- **Visual merchandiser:** creates window and interior displays in shops and department stores with the aim of increasing sales.

Further information

The Artists' Information Company	www.a-n.co.uk
Fashion jobs website	www.topfashionjobs.com
Your Creative Future (website with lots of info about creative careers)	www.yourcreativefuture.org.uk

BIOLOGY/HUMAN BIOLOGY

Biology students learn about all life on the planet – human, plant and animal. One of the things that appeals to students who consider this subject is the sheer variety involved in the syllabus, ranging from how plants get their energy, to how the human heart works and how biological systems relate to ecology and the environment. Some of the questions that A level biologists could be asked to consider include:

- What is the exact process of cell division in humans and animals?
- How does the human nervous system work in detail?
- How do viral and bacterial infections work and how does the immune system respond?
- What are ecosystems and how do they work?

Biology is a particularly popular subject at the moment because of prominent issues such as gene technology, the study of which is behind the advances in gene therapy now used by modern medicine. There may be some variation in topics according to the exam board used. Some, for instance, may put a greater emphasis on the social and environmental context of biology; all of them, however, cover the main core biological concepts.

Subject options

This subject is available at A/AS level as Biology and Human Biology. Human Biology is less frequently taught by schools and colleges, however.

The specification outlines below are based on the AQA syllabus but it's broadly similar to the content covered by the other exam boards. For an exact definition of the AS and A2 syllabus you will be studying, you should consult your school or college or even the exam board itself.

Biology

Unit 1: Core principles
Biological molecules; cells; cell transport; organisms and their environment; enzymes; digestion.

Unit 2: Genes and genetic engineering
The genetic code; the cell cycle; sexual reproduction; applications of gene technology.

Unit 3: Physiology and transport
Transport systems; the control of breathing and heartbeat; energy and exercise; the transport of substances in plants.

Unit 4: Energy, control and continuity
Energy supply; photosynthesis; respiration; survival and co-ordination; homeostasis; nervous co-ordination; analysis and integration; muscles and movement; inheritance; variation; selection and evolution; classification.

Unit 5: Environment

Energy flow and ecosystems; materials and ecosystems; studying ecosystems; dynamics and ecosystems; human activity and the environment.

Unit 6: Applied biology

Diversity; effects of pollution on diversity; adaptation; agricultural ecosystems; conservation.

Unit 7: Microbes and disease

Bacteria; biotechnology; bacterial disease; viral disease; protection against disease.

Unit 8: Behaviour and populations

Patterns of behaviour; reproductive behaviour; pregnancy; human growth and development; human populations and health.

AS students complete modules one to four; A2 students follow modules one to five and then the school or college can choose to teach one of modules six, seven or eight. Assessment is by coursework and timed examination.

Human Biology

There is some overlap with the Biology syllabus, but the material is organised differently and of course has a greater emphasis on human biology.

1.   Molecules, cells and systems

2.   Making use of biology (the practical and industrial uses of biology)

3.   Pathogens and disease

4.   Inheritance, evolution and ecosystems

5.   Physiology and the environment

6.   The human life-span (reproduction, growth, ageing).

AS students complete modules one to three; A2 students complete one to six. Assessment for both AS and A2 is by a mixture of coursework and examination.

Students normally require at least a grade C in GCSE Biology or Science to take up A level Biology and Human Biology because much of the course requires some prior knowledge. Ability in Maths and Chemistry can also be useful as students will have to collect and manipulate data, as well as understand the chemical processes that take place in the living world.

Advanced Extension Award

This level of examination is aimed at the top 10 per cent of candidates nationally. It draws on the different elements of the AS and A2 course modules and tries to assess candidates' ability to link together different aspects of biology and to communicate their knowledge effectively. For Biology, candidates take a three-hour closed examination. There are four sections and candidates must answer one question in each section. The work is externally assessed and students are awarded a Distinction or a Merit, with the Distinction being the higher mark. Students whose answers don't achieve a Merit award will receive an 'ungraded' classification. For a detailed breakdown of the assessment criteria, visit the QCA website (www.qca.org.uk).

Choosing other subjects to go with Biology

Some degree courses require at least two Science subjects so check with HE institutions' entrance criteria before choosing which subjects to study alongside Biology. Common combinations include Biology, Physics (or Maths) and Chemistry, but there is no reason why you should follow this pattern if other subjects appeal. However, if you don't want to go on to Further Education in that particular subject, then combining it with vocational subjects might be useful.

Biology at HE level

Biology at a higher level is extremely popular and there are many different biology-related courses available including biochemistry, biomedical science and genetics. Most of these related subjects would require A level Biology, but there are a few exceptions. Those who have an interest in pursuing a career in medicine, dentistry and veterinary medicine usually take Biology at A level, although this is not always necessary.

A degree in Biology?

Like most degrees these days, Biology can be quite varied and flexible in its content. However, most degrees will have some core subjects (usually studied in the first year) and then have the option of allowing students to specialise in certain areas by choosing particular modules. Sometimes degrees in this area can be called Biological Sciences often indicating a broader curriculum, but this is not always the case. Medical students can often do a degree in biomedical science or biology as part of their five-year course. Always check the precise nature of the course before you take the plunge.

Combining Biology with other degree subjects

As with most subjects, Biology can be combined with a whole range of subjects, not just those within the Sciences. Common combinations include Biology with Chemistry, Physics, Geography, Maths or Psychology. A word of warning: if you need a Biology degree for a particular job, try and check beforehand whether a combined Biology degree with another subject is acceptable.

Biology and your future career

Non-graduate jobs

Many employers requiring A levels do not really mind which subjects applicants have. In that sense, Biology A level is a good a choice as any. However, there may be some non-graduate areas of work where Biology A level is still more useful than some others. These include:

- Healthcare jobs (including nursing training)
- Some forms of laboratory work (e.g. lab assistant in a school)
- Work in a dental surgery as an assistant
- Any job requiring attention to detail and practical skills.

It's also possible to start some scientific or biology-related jobs and do training on-the-job via a night class or day release from work.

Graduate jobs directly related to Biology

If you wish to use your degree directly there are several employment areas where a degree in biology is directly relevant. Some of the most popular jobs are listed below, but further study is often required.

- **Civil Service fast streamer:** is employed by the civil service on the fast stream development programme. Uses scientific knowledge to carry out research, develop policy, manage projects and provide general administration.
- **Clinical cytogeneticist:** provides an analytical interpretation and advice service to medical staff in hospitals.
- **Industrial science researcher:** is an intellectually challenging role that can involve teamwork with other professionals, including those from other disciplines. Can involve developing new products, e.g. drugs, or new processes.
- **Life science researcher:** is employed in universities, health authorities and with some employers, e.g. pharmaceutical, healthcare products, biotechnology. Investigates and analyses natural and living phenomena, gathering scientific information and generating knowledge.
- **Medical sales executive:** represents pharmaceutical companies to general practitioners, retail pharmacists and hospital doctors. Promotes pharmaceutical products in an ethical manner.
- **Scientific lab assistants:** help scientists and others who are engaged in research, development, analysis or scientific investigations by carrying out a variety of technical and experimental tasks.
- **Secondary school teacher:** teaches the subject as a separate discipline and also have a multidisciplinary approach through integrated science teaching.

Further information

To find out more about Biology as an A level and Science in general, visit the following websites:

Advanced Biology A level   www.advancedbiology.org

Institute of Biology   www.iob.org

NHS Careers   www.nhscareers.nhs.uk

BUSINESS STUDIES

Students of business learn about organisations, how they work, as well as the different markets businesses serve. More often than not, business students will look at case studies from particular businesses and apply what they have learnt to those case studies. The kinds of questions students of this subject could consider include:

- What factors make a business successful?
- What external influences affect organisations?
- What are the different ways of motivating staff?
- How do the different functions of finance, information, human resources work together?

In essence, students gain an understanding of how organisations operate and how to make effective business decisions.

Subject options

This subject is available as a GCE A level and AS level an Advanced Extension Award, a GCE Applied A/As level, BTEC Nationals and as an NVQ. From September 2009, an Advanced Diploma in Business, Administration and Finance will also be available.

A/AS level

The outline below is based on the OCR specification. For an exact definition of the AS and A2 syllabus you will be studying, you should consult your school or college or even the exam board itself.

Businesses, their objectives and environment

How organisations are structured; internal processes; formulation of organisational objectives; how external influences affect objectives; staff motivation.

Business decisions and business behaviour

Students examine organisational issues in terms of marketing; finance and costs; human resources; and managing operations. From these perspectives students learn how organisations behave and how business decisions are made.

A2 students also complete a business project (coursework) and a unit on business strategy. Additionally, students complete one option from the following:

- Further marketing
- Further accounting and finance
- Further people in organisations
- Further operations management.

Assessment is mainly by written exam, but there is a coursework element.

Advanced Extension Award

This level of examination is aimed at the top 10 per cent of candidates nationally. It draws on the different elements of the AS and A2 course modules and tries to assess candidates' ability to link together different aspects of business and to communicate their knowledge effectively. For this subject, candidates take a three-hour closed examination. The work is externally assessed and students are awarded a Distinction or a Merit, with the Distinction being the higher mark. Students whose answers don't achieve a Merit award will receive an 'ungraded' classification. For a detailed breakdown of the assessment criteria, visit the QCA website (www.qca.org.uk). The AEA in Business is offered by OCR.

Applied A/AS level

Although there is some similarity between this course of study and the 'regular' AS/A level, the emphasis here is more on how to work effectively in business, rather than simply understanding it from an academic point of view. There is also a greater emphasis on careers within business. An outline of the specification, based on OCR's, is give below:

Level	Title of Unit	Mode of assessment
AS	Creating a marketing proposal	Portfolio
AS	Recruitment in the workplace	Portfolio
AS	Understanding the business environment	External
AS	The impact of customer service	External
AS	ICT provision in a business	Portfolio
AS	Running an enterprise activity	Portfolio
AS	Financial providers and products	Portfolio
AS	Understanding production in business	Portfolio
A2	Strategic decision-making	External
A2	A business plan for the entrepreneur	Portfolio
A2	Managerial and supervisory roles	Portfolio
A2	Launching a business online	Portfolio
A2	Promotion in action	Portfolio
A2	Constructing a financial strategy	Portfolio
A2	Launching a new product or service in Europe	Portfolio
A2	Training and development	Portfolio
A2	Business law	External
A2	Managing risk in the workplace	External

BTEC Nationals

These qualifications are aimed to give students the practical skills in business needed by the job market in that particular sector. BTEC Nationals are available in three levels (Award, Certificate and Diploma), and are offered by Edexcel exam board.

The topics available at BTEC National Award level (equivalent to one A level):

- Applied law
- Business
- Personal and Business Finance.

The topics available at BTEC National Certificate level (equivalent to two A levels):

Business	Business (Administration)	Business (E-business Software)
Business (E-business Strategy)	Business (Finance)	Business (Human Resources)
Business (Law)	Business (Management)	Business (Marketing)

The topics available at BTEC National Diploma level (equivalent to three A levels):

Business	Business (Administration)	Business (E-business Software)
Business (E-business Strategy)	Business (E-business Strategy)	Business (E-business Strategy and E-business Software)
Business (Finance)	Business (Finance and Administration)	Business (Finance and E-business Software)
Business (Finance and E-business Strategy)	Business (Finance and Human Resources)	Business (Finance and Law)
Business (Finance and Management)	Business (Finance and Marketing)	Business (Human Resources)
Business (Human Resources and Administration)	Business (Human Resources and E-business Software)	Business (Human Resources and E-business Strategy)
Business (Human Resources and Law)	Business (Human Resources and Management)	Business (Law)
Business (Law and Administration)	Business (Law and E-business Software)	Business (Law and E-business Strategy)
Business (Management and Law)	Business (Marketing)	Business (Marketing and Administration)
Business (Marketing and E-business Software)	Business (Marketing and E-business Strategy)	Business (Marketing and Human Resources)
Business (Marketing and Law)	Business (Marketing and Management)	

Assessment is by a combination of coursework, projects, case studies and examinations.

NVQ in Business

There are NVQs available in business and administration; business start-up; and business improvement. These are primarily aimed at those already working in a business environment who want to improve their on-the-job skills. Assessment is by a portfolio of evidence.

Advanced Diploma

The Advanced Diploma in Business, Administration and Finance will be available from 2009. An overview of the content of the course is given below.

Principal learning

This means you will learn all about the Diploma subject area, i.e. Business, Administration and Finance. This will be a compulsory part of the course.

Generic learning

This will involve learning functional English, mathematics, and ICT and personal, learning and thinking skills in a business context. These are vital if you want to either get a job or study at a higher level.

Project

Whatever level you are at in the Diploma, you will do a project which will be one of the main parts of your work.

Work experience

At each level of the Diploma, you will get to do 10 days' work experience.

Additional/specialist learning

This means that you can take another subject that will allow you to specialise in a particular area, depending on whether you want to get a job or go on to do further study. For example, depending on the level that you are at in the Diploma, you may choose to do a GCSE in Economics or an A level in Law, or languages, or maybe another unit from another Diploma. You may also be able to do another qualification in an area of interest or something you enjoy, like drama or sport for instance.

Levels

The BAF Diploma will be offered at 3 levels:

- Foundation – has an equivalence of four to five GCSEs at grades C and below
- Higher – has an equivalence to five to six GSCEs at grades A* to C
- Advanced – has an equivalence of three A levels.

Foundation and Higher: You will be able to study a Foundation or Higher Diploma at age 14. At the end of this two-year programme of study you have the opportunity to progress either to work, Further Education or the next Diploma level.

The Diploma will form approximately half of the National entitlement and this will give learners the opportunity to study other GCSEs, including English, Maths and Science.

Advanced: Advanced Diploma is a post-16 qualification that will be offered by schools and colleges and on completion of this, learners can progress to Higher Education or into work.

Choosing other subjects to go with Business Studies

In theory, you could combine business studies with any other subject but popular choices include Economics; Maths; Computing; Accounting; Law; Science subjects and Geography. One word of warning: if you want to study business at some of the more traditional universities, they may prefer more traditionally 'academic' subjects rather than some more 'modern' ones. Check their entry requirements before choosing.

Business Studies at HE level

Business is becoming an increasingly popular subject at HE level. The courses vary widely both in content and style. Some are very much academically focused in that they examine the theories of management; others are much more vocationally focused in that their emphasis is on the practice of management and links with the business world. You have to ask yourself which type you would prefer.

A degree in Business Studies?

At a higher level, business-related courses can be called a variety of things: Management; Business Management; Business and Finance; Business Operations and so on. Each course has a slightly different inflection so it's important to check the precise nature of each course. Most courses, however, include some core modules about business and management and then allow students to choose options over the last two years. Some courses even specify learning a foreign language as part of the course.

Combining Business Studies with other degree subjects

Popular combinations include Business and Accounting; Business and Economics; Business and Maths; Business and Law; Business and Psychology; Business and Engineering. Most employers with a strong commercial focus aren't too bothered about how you combine your degree.

Foundation degrees and Diplomas

There are many Foundation degree courses in Business and Business Management, as well as other business-related areas. Visit www.ucas.com for details of these. There are also many BTEC Higher National courses available in this area, including IT Business; Business-related Law; E-commerce; Marketing and Human Resources.

Business Studies and your future career

Non-graduate jobs

This subject will give you an insight into the business world so employers may be more likely to take you on than those have studied other things. Positions do exist in management and administration for those with A levels, especially specific programmes offered by companies in retail, banking, insurance and manufacturing.

Graduate jobs Directly related to Business Studies

A knowledge of business is useful if not essential in most careers. When recruiting for commercial or financial job opportunities, employers are prepared to consider graduates in any subject but some give preference to a business studies background, whilst others refer to this as a definite requirement.

Graduate jobs where a degree in Business Studies could be useful

Although the following occupations are open to graduates from any degree discipline, a business studies degree will provide useful background knowledge, evidence of some of the skills mentioned above and, possibly, some exemptions from papers in professional examinations.

- **Advertising account executive:** acts as a link between the client and the agency, taking responsibility for putting the proposal together and presenting it to the client. The executive co-ordinates the activities of the advertising team and administration.
- **Banking manager:** responsible for managing the daily business of a branch and for the development of new business, ensuring that sales targets are met and maintaining a customer-orientated retail team.
- **Chartered accountant:** provides financial information and maintains general accounting systems, performs audits and liaises with clients or management colleagues. Opportunities exist in industry, commerce, private practice and the public sector.
- **Distribution/logistics manager:** manages the supply, movement and storage of goods and materials. Plans, organises and co-ordinates material flow and storage through the process of manufacture from supplier to customer. Controls the total distribution operation.
- **Investment banker (corporate finance):** advises private and corporate investors about their money and currency-related activities. Also seeks to promote related financial products appropriate to the clients' needs.
- **Management consultant:** provides a professional service to business, public and other undertakings by identifying and investigating problems concerned with strategy, policy, markets, organisation, procedures and methods.
- **Marketing executive:** promotes and sells products to the public. Works on various projects to support the brand/marketing manager in developing brands and promoting existing products.

- **Personnel officer:** develops and advises on all policies relating to human resources in an organisation.
- **Public relations officer:** uses all forms of media and communications to project and protect the appropriate image of an organisation or individual.
- **Retail buyer:** successfully purchases attractive merchandise whose price, quality and availability meet customers' needs. Buyers must provide commercially viable merchandise ranges at competitive prices, whilst maximising profitability.
- **Retail manager:** in charge of the day-to-day management of a department or store; being responsible for staff, sales, customer service, effective cost control of stocks and resource management.
- **Sales executive:** promotes and maximises sales of a company's products or services in designated markets. Identifies new markets and new business and acts as liaison between producer and the retailer or wholesaler.

Further information

The Economics and Business
Education Association   www.ebea.org.uk

The Institute of Chartered Secretaries
and Administrators   www.icsa.org.uk

S. Barnes *Essential Business
Studies* (Collins)

CHEMISTRY

How can you test for the presence of acid? Why and how do substances change when you heat them? What are the properties of that changed substance? How do we express that change on paper?

These are just some of the questions A level chemists think about and explore the answers to. Some of these issues were considered at GCSE level, but A level goes into much more detail. Chemistry is about understanding the fundamental nature of life from a chemical point of view. Students learn the skills to work in a laboratory, acquire knowledge about the theories of Chemistry and test some of those theories in practice.

Subject options

This subject is available at GCE A/AS level and as an Advanced Extension Award (AEA). If you are interested in a doing a subject that is more practical and related to industry, the BTEC National course in Applied Science (Chemistry) may be worth considering.

A/AS level

The outline below is based on what the majority of exam board syllabuses include. For an exact definition of the AS and A2 syllabus you will be studying, you should consult your school or college or even the exam board itself. *NB: This subject is available at AEA level through the AQA exam board (see below).*

Atomic structure, bonding and main chemical 'groups'

Most courses go into depth about atomic structure, chemical formulae, chemical bonding and groups of chemicals such as Group 7 (chlorine to iodine).

Organic and inorganic chemistry; energetics; kinetics; qualitative equilibria

Includes the introduction to alkanes, alkenes, alcohols and halogenoalkanes; industrial inorganic chemistry; chemical reactions (endothermic and exothermic); calculating the rates of chemical reactions; understanding the dynamic nature of chemical equilibria.

Laboratory chemistry

This is all about the process of carrying out chemistry in the lab and students developing their experimental skills. Assessing students' practical skills in the lab forms an important part of every A level course.

Periodicity, quantitative equilibria and functional group chemistry

More advanced theories about chemical reactions; understanding chemical properties of certain parts of the periodic table; acids and bases; further organic chemistry (including acids, esters, carbonyl, nitrogen compounds).

Transition metals, quantitative kinetics and applied organic chemistry
Oxidisation; ionic bonding; reaction mechanisms and aromatic compounds; understanding rates of chemical reactions using quantitative techniques; learning tests to identify certain organic compounds; identifying certain chemical structures of organic compounds; using a spectrometer; understanding the importance of organic chemistry in relation to agriculture, the pharmaceutical business and other materials.

Advanced Extension Award

This level of examination is aimed at the top 10 per cent of candidates nationally. It draws on the different elements of the AS and A2 course modules and tries to assess candidates' ability to apply and communicate effectively their understanding of Chemistry, using their skills of critical analysis, evaluation, synthesis and by applying mathematical techniques to chemical contexts. Chemistry candidates take a three-hour examination which will include a total of between four and six questions. The work is externally assessed and students are awarded a Distinction or a Merit, with the Distinction being the higher mark. Students whose answers don't achieve a Merit award will receive an 'ungraded' classification. For a detailed breakdown of the assessment criteria, visit the QCA website (www.qca.org.uk).

How is A/AS level Chemistry taught and assessed?

Chemistry students learn both the theory and practice of the subject therefore they spend lots of time learning in a lab, observing practical demonstrations and carrying out supervised experiments. Depending on whether the subject is taken at AS or A2 level, exams will be taken at different points during the course. Most will be written exams but there will also be an assessed practical examination. As well as being practical, a good head for figures is also helpful to do well as this subject.

Choosing other subjects to go with Chemistry

Many students choose to combine this subject with Biology, Physics and Maths. The reason for this is that acceptance onto some degree courses require at least two Science subjects at A level. If that is not the case, then there's no reason why you can't combine Chemistry with any other subject.

Chemistry at HE level

Chemistry at HE level is extremely popular and there are many different Chemistry-related courses available including Biochemistry, Medical Biochemistry, Chemical Physics and many others. Most of these related subjects would require A level Chemistry, but there are a few exceptions. Those who have an interest in pursuing a career in medicine and dentistry, veterinary medicine usually take Chemistry at A level, although this is not always necessary.

A degree in Chemistry?

Like most degrees, Chemistry can be quite varied and flexible in its content. However, most degrees will have some core subjects (usually studied in the first year) and then have the option of allowing students to specialise in certain areas by choosing particular modules. Most degree courses expand upon the areas studied at A level and teaching involves a combination of set lectures, small-group tutorials, assigned coursework and of course work in the laboratory.

Combining Chemistry with other degree subjects

Studying Chemistry at degree level will have some overlap with other sciences. Even so, students often combine this subject with Biology or Physics. Other joint degree programmes offered by universities include:

- Chemistry with a European Language
- Chemistry with Management
- Chemistry with Maths
- Medicinal Chemistry.

Foundation degrees and Diplomas

There are some Foundation degrees in Science and specific vocational areas of Science and Chemistry such as Forensic Science for example. It is also possible to do a BTEC Higher National in Applied Chemistry where the emphasis is very much on practical applications of Chemistry for today.

Chemistry and your future career

Non-graduate jobs

Most jobs using Chemistry require higher qualifications. It may be possible, however, to get some experience working as a lab assistant, dental assistant or a veterinary assistant, but these often require further training too. Having said that, the subject is highly regarded by employers in lots of different areas of work, so students needn't just think of Chemistry-related occupations.

Graduate jobs directly related to Chemistry

- **Analytical chemist:** performs structural, quantitative, product and formulation analyses using state-of-the-art techniques, often in support of other scientists.
- **Biomedical scientist (MLSO):** carries out laboratory investigations on human samples necessary for the diagnosis, treatment and prevention of illness or disease.
- **Colour technologist:** produces dyes and pigments for the colouration of products such as textiles, paper, cosmetics and foodstuffs for highly sensitive biomedical applications and dye lasers.
- **Industrial research scientist:** organises and carries out systematic investigations to develop new products or improve existing products to meet consumer demand for quality, safety and price.

- **Materials engineer:** conducts technical investigations related to the development and production of a wide range of materials, e.g. glass, metals, polymers and plastics.
- **Process development scientist:** scales up processes developed in the laboratory so that they may be used in manufacturing large quantities. The aim is to produce products for the market in an efficient, economical and safe way.
- **Product development scientist:** takes ideas or discoveries generated by research, then develops or formulates them to the point where new products can be manufactured. The work may be to develop new products or to improve the performance of existing ones.
- **Quality assurance officer:** develops and applies tests to ensure raw materials, intermediates and finished products meet specified standards of composition, texture, taste, appearance and performance.
- **Research scientist (physical sciences):** plans and conducts experimental research, evaluates ideas, uses and develops theoretical knowledge in either theoretical or applied areas.
- **Secondary school teacher, Further Education lecturer, or Higher Education lecturer:** teaches chemistry in schools or colleges of Further Education. Lecturers in Higher Education balance their teaching load with research and supervision of postgraduate researchers.

Graduate jobs where a degree in Chemistry could be useful

- **Clinical biochemist:** carries out tests on samples from patients to assist with the investigation, diagnosis and treatment of disease. Liaises with clinicians on interpretation of results.
- **Forensic scientist:** analyses samples in relation to crime. Writes reports which are presented as evidence in courts.
- **(Medical) sales executive:** negotiates sales and generates new business between producers and their clients, either business to general public or, more likely, business to business.
- **Patent agent:** acts as an agent for inventors or companies with new ideas or processes to protect the intellectual property for the client.
- **Scientific journalist:** researches and writes scientific news and articles for the general public or for more specialist audiences.
- **Toxicologist:** carries out and interprets laboratory and field studies to identify toxins and their effect on living systems and the environment.

Further information

Chemistry and Industry magazine online	www.chemind.org
Chemsoc careers	www.chemsoc.org.uk
Royal Society of Chemistry	www.rsc.org

CLASSICAL CIVILISATION

This subject is about the civilisation of Ancient Rome and Greece. It allows students who don't have knowledge of the Greek and Latin Languages to gain an appreciation of culture during the period 1500BC to AD450. To study Classical Civilisation means to study the politics, art, philosophy and literature of the time and geographical settings.

Subject options

This subject is available at GCE A level, offered by the OCR exam board. Related subjects available through OCR include Classics, Classical Greek, Classics: Ancient History and Classics: Latin. Latin is also offered by OCR at Advanced Extension Award (AEA) level.

A level Classical Civilisation

The outline below is broadly based on the OCR specification.

Greek and Roman literature (Epics, Tragedy, Comedy and Satire)
A great emphasis of the course is given to the literature of the time including:

- *The Illiad* and Virgil's *Aeneid* (Greek and Roman Epics)
- The works of Aeschylus, Sophocles and Euripides (Greek Tragedy)
- The works Aristophanes, Horace, Juvenal and Pliny (Greek Comedy and Roman Satire).

Greek and Roman history
As well as literature, students are asked to consider the historical writings of the time including:

- The works of Herodotus and Thucydides (Greek)
- The writings of Tacitus and Suetonius (Roman).

Additionally, there is usually some emphasis on the Roman occupation of Britain and students scrutinise written evidence about it.

Greek art and architecture
Students learn how to assess the importance of Greek art and architecture and how it reflects the society of its time.

Approaches to archaeology and Roman sites and artefacts
In this module students learn the definition of archaeology, archaeological methods and practice, archaeological principles and how to interpret archaeological evidence. They also learn about artefacts originating from Roman Britain.

How is A/AS level Classical Civilisation taught and assessed?

Students learn by examining a range of writing (usually in translation) from the period in question. There may be some opportunities to visit a Roman or Greek site of archaeological interest. Most of the assessment is carried out by written exams over the two years but there is also a course work option as well.

Choosing other subjects to go with Classical Civilisation

This A level overlaps with many disciplines and would be combined well with Literature, Ancient History, Philosophy, Archaeology, History and many others. But, like most subjects, it can be combined with any other subjects including the Sciences.

Classical Civilisation at HE level

There may be some courses called Classical Civilisation at HE level but most will probably be called Classics or Classical Studies. For entry onto an HE course, An A level in Classics or Classical Civilisation is not normally needed but good grades in traditional arts and/or humanities subjects would stand you in good stead.

A degree in Classics/Classical Civilisation?

Most degree courses in this area called Classics, and like A level Classical Studies, the focus of most degree courses will be on Ancient Roman and Greek history and civilisation. However, this will be much more wide-ranging and in much more depth. There may also be a requirement for students to become familiar with written Greek and Latin so that they can analyse historical documents in the original language.

Combining Classics with other degree subjects

Classics cuts across quite a few disciplines so it's quite common to see it combined with other subjects. Some joint programmes offered by universities include:

- Classics and Applied Computing
- Classical Studies and French
- Classical Studies and Philosophy
- War Studies and Classical Studies
- Classical Studies with Film Studies.

These are just a few examples, but there are many other possible combinations.

Classics and your future career

Non-graduate jobs

This A level will give you lots of marketable skills for a variety of jobs, even though you probably won't be able to use the knowledge which you've learned. Skills you can gain from this course include the ability to research, form judgements, analyse information and empathy.

Graduate jobs directly related to Classics

There are only a few jobs which are directly related to a classics degree. For the following occupations a degree in a classical subject is essential.

Secondary school teacher: there are a few Postgraduate Certificate in Education (PGCE) courses for graduates wanting to teach Classics in state secondary schools. Opportunities also exist in primary schools, independent schools, sixth form colleges and Further or Higher Education.

Graduate jobs where Classics could be useful

Jobs where the transferable skills learned from a classics background are particularly useful include the following.

- **Administration:** planning and organising services, providing information and collecting data to form the basis for future actions within the organisation, informing the world outside the organisation. You could work in public service; industry (company secretary); education; health service; charities; voluntary or international organisations.
- **Archivist:** reserves, stores and safeguards records for permanent retention. Makes records accessible for administrative or historical research purposes. Latin is necessary for work with older archives.
- **Civil Service fast Streamer:** involves policy making (administrative trainee) or general management (staffing, finance, immigration, consular work) roles within embassies or high commissions abroad and in the Foreign and Commonwealth Office in London.
- **Editor:** copy editing of classical typescripts. Checking the text reads fluently, aptly and is translated correctly. Ensuring internal consistency and that the text is free from errors of language, spelling or punctuation.
- **Museum/art gallery curator:** the collection, documentation, preservation, display and interpretation of materials for public benefit.
- **Solicitor:** prepares deeds and contracts of all types, manages legal cases, instructs counsel (i.e. barristers) in the higher courts and acts as an advocate for others in the lower courts. You could work in private practice as a generalist or specialist, in industry, public service, law centres, magistrate's courts or the armed services.
- **Technical author:** preparing technical information for publication in a way that is intelligible to a wide range of users. You need to produce clear, logical, unambiguous and accurate text. You must be able to communicate effectively with very different people from engineers to school children.

Further information

The Council for British Archaeology	www.britarch.ac.uk
Current Archaeology	www.archaeology.co.uk
The Institute of Conversation	www.icon.org.uk

COMMUNICATION AND CULTURE

What is culture and communication? How do we communicate effectively? How is culture communicated through the media? What is the difference between high culture and popular culture? How does culture relate to capitalism, globalisation and consumerism? These are some of the questions that students of communication could consider. The formal study of this subject is about the theory and practice of communication and culture and how they interconnect.

Subject options

Although Communication Studies is still being taught until 2009, this subject will be replaced by GCE A/AS Communication and Culture and will be offered by the AQA exam board.

Main elements of the course

The outline below is based on the AQA syllabus.

Unit 1: Understanding communication and culture

The nature of culture; definitions of culture; the meanings and practices of everyday life; high culture and popular culture; the relationship between culture and value; verbal and non-verbal communication; identity and self-presentation; group communication; reading images and products.

Unit 2: The individual and contemporary culture: portfolio

This is a piece of individual work based on one of the following topics: communication, culture and the individual; cultural contexts and practices.

Unit 3: Communicating culture

A study of a cultural site; dominant and alternative approaches to the understanding of communication and culture; the relationship of capitalism, globalisation and consumerism to cultural products and practices; key concepts and cultural issues.

Unit 4: Further aspects of communication and culture

A major piece of independent work; personal and social identities; social and cultural rituals.

AS students complete units one and two; A2 students complete units one to four. Assessment is by a combination of coursework, case studies, presentations and closed examinations.

Choosing other subjects to go with Communication and Culture

Communication studies obviously lends itself to be combined with subjects such as English Literature, Drama, Media Studies, History and Sociology but it can be combined with almost any subject. It is a new GCE subject, so if you hope to go on to Higher Education, make sure it is seen as an acceptable subject in terms of entrance criteria for degree courses.

Communication and Culture at HE level

You have a few choices if you want to study this subject at HE level. There are degree courses in Communication, Culture and the Media; there are others solely in Communication Studies and yet others focused purely on Cultural Studies. Choose the one you will find most interesting!

A degree in Communication and Culture?

A degree in Communication and Culture Studies focuses on the communicative and cultural activities that shape the worlds we live in: everyday life; human interaction; global relations and technological mediations. Courses focus on three main strands: communication in contemporary culture; communication in human interactions; and global contexts and communication media.

Combining Communication and Culture with other degree subjects

Subjects that can be combined well with this subject include English; Media Studies; Philosophy; History; Sociology; Linguistics and Politics.

Foundation degrees and Diplomas

There is not a specific Foundation degree in Communication and Culture, but there are some related to Media Studies, of which Communication Studies forms an important part. Currently there is no BTEC Higher National in Communication Studies.

Communication and Culture and your future career

Non-graduate jobs

An A level in Communication Studies will give you skills in communicating effectively, the ability to analyse issues, critically evaluate pieces of writing and an awareness of popular culture. These skills may enable you to get junior positions in advertising, marketing, public relations, the media and other areas of business.

Graduate jobs directly related to Communication and Culture

Many students on these courses are interested in gaining employment in all aspects of the media industry. Careers in the media, however, are highly sought after and competition is likely to be fierce.

- **Broadcast assistant, radio:** assists with production and presentation of programmes for local and national radio stations.

- **Broadcasting presenter:** fronts the programme, specific responsibilities vary depending on the programme.
- **Journalism:** reports on news and other areas of interests for newspapers, periodicals, radio and TV.
- **Multimedia programmer:** researches, develops and produces materials for new media based company activities.
- **Programme researcher, broadcasting/film/video:** acts as an assistant producer with responsibility for conception and implementation of a programme.
- **Radio producer:** responsible for initiating ideas, selling these to commissioning editors and managing the technical and creative team to produce the final programme.
- **Television/film/video producer:** undertakes the artistic interpretation of materials and directs the production of shows/films.
- **Television production assistant:** provides organisational and secretarial services for programme director.

Graduate jobs where Communication and Culture could be useful

- **Advertising account executive:** takes overall responsibility for co-ordination, planning and organisation of advertising campaigns.
- **Editorial assistant:** assists editorial staff in the commissioning, planning and production of books, journals and magazines.
- **Event organiser:** identifies potential business, researches, writes, plans and runs all types of conferences on behalf of a client or own organisation.
- **Information officer/manager:** ensures effective communication of information relating to a particular field of interest.
- **Market research executive:** undertakes systematic research to determine the potential market for a product or service.
- **Public relations account executive:** PR agencies work for their clients in presenting their image to the public. They decide on strategies to be used and which media would be the most effective.

Further information

Skillset   www.skillset.org; www.skillsformedia.com

COMPUTING

Computers are more central to our lives than ever before. We use them at home and at work for a variety of different purposes. Students of Computing will not only get a better understanding of how computers work but how computers and information systems are used to solve organisational problems as well as how they are used in other areas of life. How do you design and implement a computer system? What's the most appropriate IT application for this situation? These are just some of the questions that students of this subject are asked to consider.

Subject options

This subject is available at A/AS level, and as BTEC Nationals. Some students may also be interested in a related subject – Information, Communication and Technology (ICT) – which is available as a 'regular' and applied A/AS level. The main difference between A level Computing and ICT is that Computing focuses solely on computers and software and is slightly more theoretical. ICT considers the broader context of how we use information and technology, of which computers are a big part.

From September 2008, there will also be an Advanced Diploma in IT available, please see page 129 for more detail.

A/AS level

The outline below is based on what the majority of exam board syllabuses include. For an exact definition of the AS and A2 syllabus you will be studying, you should consult your school or college or even the exam board itself. Students taking the AS award only will have to study about 50 per cent of the modules which are needed for the full A2 award.

Computer systems

In this module students learn about the many different applications of computer systems; the social, legal and economic implications of IT; the different types of data files and data security; software and hardware; networking and maintenance.

Design and organisation of information systems

Students learn what constitutes and information system; whether an information system is suitable for computerisation; organising data; designing and implementing software.

Computer systems designs

Understanding databases; organising files; understanding hardware and software; networks and communications.

Systems development

Different ways of implementing an information system; project management; managing information; data structures; programming.

BTEC Nationals

These qualifications are aimed to give students the practical skills in computing needed by the job market in that particular sector. BTEC Nationals in IT and Computing are available in three levels, and are offered by Edexcel exam board:

- BTEC National Award (equivalent to one GCE A level)
- BTEC National Certificate (equivalent to two GCE A levels)
- BTEC National Diploma (equivalent to three GCE A levels).

The topics available at BTEC National Award level are:

- Applied Law
- Business
- Personal and Business Finance.

The subjects available at BTEC National Certificate and Diploma level are:

IT practitioners (IT and Business)	IT practitioners (Networking)
IT practitioners (Systems Support)	IT practitioners (Software Development)

Assessment is by a combination of coursework, projects, case studies and examinations.

NVQs in Information Technology

There are Level 3 NVQs available in this subject, aimed at IT users and IT professionals. Both assume that those taking the qualification are working with computers as part of their job. The NVQ qualifications could be of interest to those who want to start work after their GCSEs.

How is A/AS level Computing taught and assessed?

Case studies make up much of the teaching methods of this course – students work with them to see generate IT-based solutions for business problems or scenarios. Students usually have to do two projects (one at AS stage and the other at A2 stage) probably on system design and/or software development. The rest of the assessment is by written exams at various points in the course. Although you don't need your own computer as your school or college should have them, it will help when it comes to independent work at home.

Choosing other subjects to go with Computing

Subjects chosen to combine with computing and IT include Maths; Management; Business; Law; Accounting and many others. Bear in mind that you may not need Computing A level to study it at degree level.

Computing at HE level

There are very many IT related courses available at HE level. Some are very theoretical; others are very practical or applied in their emphasis. Computer Science tends to be more academic and theoretical whereas Computer Studies tends to be more practical. You should always check the specific nature of a course before applying.

A degree in Computing?

Most computing courses, even if they are theoretical, will consider how IT is applied to business, industry and research. There are usually core components in the first year with some flexibility in the final two years depending on your interests. The kinds of issues considered include:

- Bioinformatics
- Communications and networks
- Computational finance
- Information security
- Logic programming
- Object-oriented modelling
- Object-oriented software engineering
- Web and internet technologies.

Assessment is via a combination of final exams, coursework and project work.

Combining Computing with other degree subjects

The different combinations possible with the subject are numerous, but some joint programmes offered by some IT/Computer Science Departments at university include:

- Computer Science with Artificial Intelligence
- Computer Science with French
- Computer Science with Management
- Computer Science and Maths
- Computer Science and Physics.

Foundation degrees and Diplomas

There are many Foundation degrees in IT-related subjects, examples being Business Information Technology, Web Development, Design for Digital Technologies and many more. Find a course at www.ucas.com. There are also BTEC Higher Nationals offered in Computing.

Computing and your future career

Non-graduate jobs

Given that nearly every organisation needs computers now, you will be an asset if you have an advanced understanding of them. In that sense, there are quite a few junior positions that you could apply for. You may even be able to get work in IT support in some organisations without any further qualifications.

Graduate jobs directly related to Computing

- **Applications developer:** writes and modifies programs to enable a computer to carry out specific tasks, such as stock control or payroll, typically for technical, commercial and business users.
- **Database administrator:** responsible for the usage, accuracy, efficiency, security, maintenance and development of an organisation's computerised databases.
- **Information technology consultant:** gives independent and objective advice on how best to use information technology to solve business problems. The work includes analysing problems, making recommendations and implementing new systems.
- **Software engineer:** specifies, develops, documents and maintains computer software programs in order to meet client or employer need. Usually works as part of a team.
- **Systems designer:** takes the specification for the requirements of a computer system and designs the system including hardware, software, communications, installation, testing and maintenance.
- **Systems developer:** sets up the computer operating systems and standard software services essential to the operation of any computer.

Graduate jobs where Computing Could be useful

The following jobs will make some use of your IT background.

- **IT sales professional:** sells computer hardware, software and peripherals; normally works in conjunction with sales representatives for a computer manufacturer.
- **Magazine journalist:** researches and writes news and feature articles which are suited to the magazine's reader profile.
- **Recruitment consultant:** particularly for the IT sector. Brings together jobseekers with vacancies on behalf of an employer.
- **Secondary school teacher:** teaches one, or more, specialist subject/s to classes of secondary pupils aged 11–18. IT is currently a shortage subject.

Further information

The British Computer Society   www.bcs.org

The Computer Information Centre   www.compinfo-center.com

P. Heathcote *A Level Computing*
(Payne-Gallway, 2004)

CRITICAL THINKING

Critical Thinking is a bit different from most subjects in that it is not a single discipline. Students who take this subject will learn how to think about issues in a variety of different ways and develop critical reasoning skills. Among other things, you will learn how to construct an argument and how to see the flaws in other people's, testing hypotheses and different ways of making decisions. The course will prepare you for HE, employment and the general demands of daily living.

Subject options

This subject is available as GCE A/AS level and is offered as an Advanced Extension Award (AEA).

A/AS level

The outline below is based on the AQA specification

Unit 1: Foundation unit

How to recognise reasoned argument and its contexts; interpreting and evaluating reasoning; identifying evidence, ambiguity and persuasive language within reasoning; recognising bad reasoning and countering it with cogent responses; the basic vocabulary of reasoning.

Unit 2: Information, inference and explanation

Presenting evidence and information; numerical and statistical reasoning; patterns and correlations; plausible explanations; making inferences from evidence; using data and information to construct arguments.

Unit 3: Beliefs, claims and arguments

Knowledge, belief and their relevance to critical thinking; evidence, beliefs and claims to knowledge; testing hypotheses; patterns of reasoning, logic, ethics, principles and rhetoric.

Unit 4: Reasoning and decision making

Reasoned decision making; using information to assess and identify consequences; value-based decision making; assessing, judging and evaluating arguments.

Teaching is mainly classroom based but there may be some case study work, which also forms part of the exam. Assessment is by written papers.

Advanced Extension Award

This course is for the most able students (the top 10 per cent). It allows them to show a greater depth of understanding than they need for A level alone. Students complete a three-hour examination in which they are presented with various pieces of information and some questions based on them. Students will not require any prior knowledge to complete this AEA, but they will need to use the critical thinking skills they've developed from the A level course and to apply them to the following contexts:

- Society, politics and the economy
- Science and Technology
- Mathematics and associated reasoning skills
- The humanities
- The arts.

Choosing other subjects to go with Critical Thinking

NB: Some universities may not recognise Critical Thinking as a qualifying subject – always check with the HE institution concerned.

Subjects that go will include Philosophy, Law and Mathematics.

Critical Thinking at HE level

Given that critical thinking is an important skill needed for most HE courses, there are no specific degree programmes in it. However, students interested in this subject might be particularly attracted to subjects such as Philosophy and Law.

Foundation degrees and Diplomas

There are no Foundation degrees and BTEC Higher Nationals in this subject.

Critical Thinking and your future career

There are specific jobs related to this subject but employers appreciate people who have a broad base of knowledge and who can think for themselves. Critical Thinking aims to equip students with both of these things. However, like many universities, some employers might not recognise Critical Thinking as a 'legitimate' A/AS level subject.

Further information

www.criticalthinking.org.uk

DESIGN AND TECHNOLOGY

Students of this subject learn all about the ways products in society are designed, created and implemented. At one end of the spectrum this may the creative and artistic design process; at the other it may be design and technology in an industrial context. Students also gain a critical understanding of the influences of design and technology processes from a historical perspective and in current practice. In particular, the use of information technology is also emphasised as a way of enhancing design and technology processes. As a student of Design and Technology, you will also be encouraged to use your own creativity and innovative skills to produce your own high quality products.

Subject options

This subject is available at GCE A/AS level. *NB: Some exam boards will offer different A levels in different aspects of Design and Technology such as Food Technology and Systems Control Technology.*

Also, from September 2009, there will be an Advanced Diploma in Manufacturing and Product Design available.

A/AS level

The outline below is based on what the majority of exam board syllabuses include. For an exact definition of the syllabus you will be studying, you should consult your school or college or even the exam board itself.

Industrial and commercial products and practices
Learning how to create design specifications; understanding the different characteristics of a range of materials; large scale manufacturing processes; quality control; estimating the potential appeal of a product; health and safety issues.

Product development
Students have to complete independent project work in relation to developing a product.

Materials, components and systems
Classification of materials (e.g. ferrous and non-ferrous) and components (e.g. rivets, nuts, bolts, etc.); preparing and testing materials; computer-aided design (CAD); the use of IT in the manufacturing process.

Design and Technology capability
This is a synoptic unit where students have to make connections from all they've learned so far. The particular emphasis is on the step-by-step process of creating a workable and marketable design and product.

Advanced Diploma

Available to study from September 2009, the Diploma in Manufacturing and Product Design contains four key areas of learning.

Principal learning

This is sector-specific learning. For example with the Manufacturing Diploma students will develop knowledge, understanding and the skills relevant to the manufacturing sub-sectors. You will also be given opportunities to apply these skills to work based roles or situations.

Generic learning

All students taking part on a Diploma will still study core subjects including English, Maths, Science and ICT, PE and citizenship.

Work experience

The Diploma in Manufacturing and Product Design will also incorporate a minimum of 10 days' work experience.

Additional/Specialist learning

You will be able to choose from a range of learning options selected by employers as being beneficial to working in the different manufacturing industry. This could cover areas such as health and safety or quality assurance.

Levels

Foundation Diploma in Manufacturing and Product Design (ages 14–16) will be broadly comparable, in terms of average length of study, to a programme of four to five GCSEs. This will provide students with the opportunity to explore the full range of manufacturing sub-sectors. Students will benefit from an introduction to the manufacturing sub-sectors with the emphasis on building basic skills in terms of industry knowledge and the application of practical skills generic to manufacturing.

Higher Diploma in Manufacturing and Product Design (ages 14–16 or 16–18) is broadly comparable, in terms of average length of study, to a programme of five to six GCSEs. Students will be encouraged to further explore a range of practical skills and to develop a broad underpinning knowledge of manufacturing practices and processes. You will gain experience in a wide range of transferable skills such as critical thinking and problem solving, and develop basic practical skills to apply your learning.

Advanced Diploma in Manufacturing and Product Design (ages 16–18) is broadly comparable, in terms of average length of study, to a programme of three GCE A levels. A subset award comparable to two A levels will also be available and known as the Progression Diploma. This will allow students to refine their skills and knowledge by offering an opportunity to specialise and explore fewer sectors at a deeper level. The content will remain broad with links across manufacturing sectors to allow progression into employment, further HE/FE education or on to an apprenticeship.

How is A/AS level Design and Technology taught and assessed?

This subject is taught by a mixture of teacher-led activities and 'hands-on' practical work. Students have to work to design briefs and produce portfolios and projects throughout the two years. The amount depends on whether you are an AS or A2 candidate. At least 40 per cent of the assessment marks are based on practical coursework and the rest will be assessed by written exams at various points in the course. To do well in this subject you will need a practical mind, good business sense and creative flair.

Choosing other subjects to go with Design and Technology

There are many possibilities to combine this subject with others. Those with an artistic bent could choose A levels in the creative field and those who are more interested in the technical side could consider other subjects such as Engineering, Computing and Manufacturing.

Design and Technology at HE level

Those with an A level in this subject could be drawn to a whole range of HE courses such as architecture, product design, engineering and IT. Courses in Design and Technology have different emphases but most have strong links with industry, with some offering a sandwich placement as part of the course. Art or technology-related subjects are usually preferred but not essential.

A degree in Design and Technology?

Like many courses, this one tends to include core courses and some optional ones in years 2 and 3. Some of the following modules may appear in university courses:

- Computing for designers
- Computer-aided modelling
- Design for sustainable development
- Design practice
- Electronic systems
- Internet and interface for designers
- Management and marketing
- Materials science and processing
- Universal design.

Combining Design and Technology with other degree subjects

Many courses in Design and Technology have different focuses (e.g. computer-aided design, engineering product design, product design and management and so on). This may affect the subjects that students would like to combine with design and technology.

Foundation degrees and Diplomas

Foundation degrees exist in specific areas of Design and Technology, especially in relation to creative arts and design and engineering. Visit www.ucas.com to find one. While there are no specific BTEC Higher Nationals in Design and Technology, they do exist in 3D Design and Graphic Design.

Design and Technology and your future career

Non-graduate jobs

Apprenticeships are a possibility in construction, manufacturing or engineering. It may also be possible to get junior positions (technician level) in computer-aided design or engineering.

Graduate jobs directly related to Design and Technology

- **Exhibition/display designer:** organises the design of exhibition and display stands. Liaises with clients to produce designs that communicate their desired messages.
- **Fashion clothing designer:** produces designs for clothing and accessories. May specialise in an area such as sportswear.
- **Production engineering:** planning, managing and maintaining production methods and processes to make the most efficient use of resources.
- **Production manager:** organising and scheduling production, selecting and controlling process variables, setting and meeting targets and people management.
- **Quality assurance officer:** establishing and operating systems that ensure quality standards in products, packing, delivery, labelling, etc. Also involves trouble-shooting and technical investigations.
- **Technical sales engineer:** technical advisory work, sales and after sales service.
- **Textile designer:** creates designs in knit, weave or print to be used in the production of fabric or textile products.

Graduate jobs where a degree in Design and Technology could be useful

- **Advertising art director:** creates visual ideas to be used within advertising. Works as part of a team alongside illustrators, photographers and those responsible for editorial. Can involve any media.
- **Information scientist:** finding, storing, evaluating and disseminating scientific, technical and commercial information.
- **Information technology and management services** (industrial engineering, work study, IT, systems, etc): investigating business, commercial, industrial problems and data processing requirements.

Further information

The Design Council   www.designcouncil.org.uk

E. Norman et al. *Advanced Design and Technology* (Longman)

DRAMA AND THEATRE STUDIES

As a student of A level Drama and Theatre Studies you will have the opportunity develop your skills of performance in many different areas. You will also gain a greater understanding of the how playwrights use certain techniques to enable their plays to come to life on the stage. The skills gained while studying this course will give a good start for a career in the theatre, but equally it is a good all-round subject for those who simply want to deepen their interest and enjoyment of the area.

Subject options

This subject is available at GCE A/AS level. Edexcel, AQA and WJEC currently offer this A/AS level, although OCR offers a course in Performance Studies.

Some students may also be interested in the new Advanced Diploma in Creative and Media, available from September 2008. Please see page 147 for further details.

A/AS level

For an exact definition of the AS and A2 syllabus you will be studying, you should consult your school, college or the exam board itself. The following outline is based largely on the Edexcel A/AS level syllabus.

Unit 1: Exploration of drama and theatre
You study two plays chosen by your school or college.

Unit 2: Text in performance I
You will be examined on your acting or design skills within a directed production of a play

Unit 3: Text in context I
You will have to demonstrate your understanding of the play used in Unit 2 as well as another seen in performance.

Unit 4: devising
Students learn how to devise an original piece of theatre for presentation to an audience.

Unit 5: Text in performance II
Here you will study a further play in depth from the viewpoint of a designer, director or performer.

Unit 6: Texts in context II
This unit requires the study of two prescribed plays in detail. You will have to examine the plays from different points of views and make connections between them, building on what you've learned from the previous units.

Students who intend to complete the full AS + A2 course complete all six units. Those going only for the A2 complete modules one to three.

How is A/AS level Drama and Theatre Studies taught and assessed?

There is some classroom learning as part of the course but you will also be spending a lot of time doing practical performance work, possibly in a drama studio. A good grade at GCSE Literature would help you with this course but it's not always a prerequisite. Assessment is by a combination of written exams, coursework and assessed performances.

Choosing other subjects to go with Drama and Theatre Studies

Good companions for this subject include English Literature, Media Studies, History and perhaps Performing Arts. Be aware of any overlaps between subjects and check the admissions criteria of universities if you want to study at a higher level.

Drama and Theatre Studies at HE level

There are many different types of Theatre Studies-related courses out there. Some specialise in particular aspects of drama and theatre such as performance, directing, stage design, lighting and so on. Others go for a broad overview of drama and the theatre. You have to ask yourself, which one would suit you more? Some courses include a year abroad at another university.

A degree in Drama and Theatre Studies?

Some sample degree modules from a typical degree programme in this area might include:

- Critical theories I & II
- Elements of performance I & II
- Explorations in space
- Practical skills
- Staging histories
- Writing and performance.

Combining Drama and Theatre studies with other degree subjects

This subject is offered in combination with English Literature, a modern language, History, Media Studies and many more.

Foundation degrees and Diplomas

BTEC Higher Nationals exist in specific areas of the Theatre and Performing Arts. There are also a number of Foundation degree courses in many different aspects of performing arts. You can search for them at www.ucas.com.

Drama and Theatre Studies and your future career

Non-graduate jobs

If you want a career in performance or in the technical side of the theatre, you will probably have to go and do further study. It's possible to get your foot in the door straight after A levels though, by working in an administrative role within a theatre within the box office, for instance.

Graduate jobs directly related to Drama and Theatre Studies

The availability of some of the following jobs may depend on the type of degree you've done and relevant work experience. Some related jobs will require relevant postgraduate study and if you want to become a performer you may need further professional training.

- **Actor:** using speech, body language and movement, an actor communicates a character and situations to an audience.
- **Drama therapist:** using drama to treat or educate people with health or emotional difficulties through therapeutic techniques.
- **Secondary school teacher:** teaching drama, music or other curriculum subjects in schools and colleges.
- **Theatre director:** co-ordinates all the artistic aspects of a dramatic presentation from inception, through production stages and rehearsals, to the final performance.
- **Theatre stage manager**: organises and co-ordinates rehearsals and performances and liaises between the director and the technical staff.
- **Wardrobe manager**: supervises the making, buying, hiring and maintenance of costumes, accessories and wigs and controls the budget for all these items.

Graduate jobs where a degree in Drama and Theatre Studies could be useful

- **Arts administrator:** facilitates the planning and promotion of visual and performing arts activities, sometimes specialising in areas such as finance and marketing.
- **Community arts worker:** concerned with the promotion of the arts in the community often through working with young people in schools and youth centres.
- **Journalist:** there are many specialist publications covering the arts but entry is very competitive. Graduates could start in mainstream broadcast or print journalism and specialise or become freelance later.
- **Programme researcher:** supports the producer by helping to organise and plan the programme.

- **Television production assistant:** organises and coordinates programme activities, booking performers and facilities and providing administrative support.

Further information

Equity (Actors Union)   www.equity.org.uk

National Association of Youth Theatres   www.nayt.org.uk

National Council for Drama Training   www.ncdt.co.uk

M. Banham (ed.) *The Cambridge Guide to Theatre* (Cambridge University Press)

ECONOMICS

As a student of Economics, you will learn about how the markets work, what factors affect them and make them crash or fail. You will also consider how economies develop, the place of the UK in the global market and economies are managed by countries. On a more specific level, students may consider how economic forces affect things such as house prices, petrol prices and the price of a range of consumable goods. Students become familiar with concepts such as inflation, balance of payments and the pros and cons of a single European currency!

Subject options

Economics is available at GCE A/AS level and as an Advanced Extension Award (AEA). Edexcel also offers GCE A/AS level in Economics and Business Studies.

A/AS level

The outline below is based on what the majority of exam board syllabuses include. For an exact definition of the syllabus you will be studying, you should consult your school or college or even the exam board itself.

Your course will cover most or all of the following:

- Economic development
- Industrial economics
- Labour markets
- Managing the economy
- Markets – how they work
- Markets – why they fail
- The UK in the global economy.

Much of the subject is teacher-led in the classroom but students may also consider case studies, TV programmes, analyse newspaper reports and analyse charts, graphs and tables. Students should have a good head for figures and possess could analytical skills. A good grade in GCSE Maths will help you in this area. Assessment is mainly by written exam at various points in the course although there may be some element of coursework too.

Advanced Extension Award

This level of examination is aimed at the top 10 per cent of candidates nationally. It draws on the different elements of the AS and A2 course modules and tries to assess candidates' ability to apply and communicate effectively their understanding of Economics using their skills of critical analysis, evaluation, synthesis and by applying economic concepts to different contexts. Assessment is by a closed examination and the work is externally assessed and students are awarded a Distinction or a Merit, with the Distinction being the higher mark. Students whose answers don't achieve a Merit award will receive an 'ungraded' classification. For a detailed breakdown of the assessment criteria, visit the QCA website (www.qca.org.uk).

A/AS level Economics and Business Studies

This subject looks at the relationship between the two subjects. More specifically, it applies Economics concepts to thinking about business issues. Topics covered include:

- Competition, markets, supply and price
- Elasticity of demand
- How exchange rates affect businesses
- Profit margins
- Purchasing patterns
- What do customers want?.

Assessment is by a mixture of closed examinations and coursework.

Choosing other subjects to go with Economics

Popular choices to combine with Economics include History, Mathematics, Computing, Management/Business, but like most subjects it can be combined with any A level discipline.

Economics at HE level

Some degree courses are very mathematical, so A level Maths will be just as useful as A level Economics if you want to do a degree in the subject. The most prestigious courses, such as the one offered by the London School of Economics (LSE), will demand the very highest A level grades to get a place. Having said that, Economics is a subject offered by many institutions so it should be possible to get a place with lower grades.

A degree in Economics?

There is some variation in Economics degrees around the country but most of them have some of the common core subjects which include:

- Economics
- Elementary statistical theory
- Macroeconomic principles
- Mathematical methods
- Microeconomic principles
- Principles of econometrics.

There may also be some optional papers in the second and/or third year such as:

- Africa and the world economy
- Europe and the global economy

- Further mathematical methods (calculus) game theory
- Locational change and business activity
- Managerial accounting
- Operational research methods
- Philosophy of economics
- The politics of international economic relations.

Combining Economics with other degree subjects

Very well-known combinations include Philosophy, Politics and Economics (PPE), Economics with History, Maths and Economics, Business Management with Economics, Economics with Law. Economics with a foreign language is also becoming more common. If you intend to work as an economist, however, it's probably safer in career terms to do pure Economics.

Foundation degrees and Diplomas

There are no Foundation degrees specifically in Economics, but there are some in Business Administration and Management which may have some overlap with elements of Economics. Similarly, while there are BTEC Higher Nationals in Business, none exist purely in Economics.

Economics and your future career

Non-graduate jobs

A level Economics is highly regarded by employers and should stand you in good stead should decide to start your career without going on to further study. Banks, retail organisations, insurance companies and some areas of City and financial services take people on with good A levels, although some jobs are only accessible via a degree.

Graduate jobs directly related to Economics

The role of economist is probably the most obvious work area directly related to your course. Most economists are concerned with practical applications of economic policy. They use their understanding of economic relationships to advise businesses and other organisations including insurance companies, banks, securities firms, industry and trade associations, unions and government agencies. Entry to the profession is very competitive. Successful candidates tend to have a strong academic record and, often, a higher degree as well.

Graduate jobs where a degree in Economics could be useful

- **Accountancy:** providing financial information and maintaining general accounting systems, performing audits and liasing with clients or management colleagues. Opportunities exist in industry, commerce, private practice and the public sector.

- **Actuarial work:** assessing probabilities and risk traditionally in the insurance and pensions sectors, although increasingly in other areas. Requires strong mathematical and statistical skills.
- **Corporate, commercial and investment banking:** providing a broad range of financial services and advice to companies, institutions and governments. This includes dealing with mergers and acquisitions; arranging or underwriting equity or debt issues; identifying and securing new deals with clients.
- **Insurance underwriter:** assesses risks and premiums to be charged, liaises with clients and brokers. Other insurance industry roles, such as broking, claims and sales are likely to involve more client contact.
- **Investment analyst:** undertakes research to provide ideas and information to fund managers. The information that they provide enables the fund manager to make decisions relating to the investment portfolios that they manage.
- **Management consultancy:** advising private and public sector organisations on business issues. Management consultants are primarily concerned with initiating and implementing technological, organisational and behavioural change.
- **Market research executive:** conducts or commissions market research by planning and controlling projects usually for independent research agencies.
- **Political party research officer:** responsible for making sure that the party for which they work is able to develop realistic new policies in response to, or in anticipation of, changing social, political and economic conditions.
- **Statistician:** concerned with the collection, analysis, interpretation and presentation of quantitative information. Statisticians design samples, collect data using a variety of methods, process data and advise on the strengths and limitations of results.
- **Trader:** involves undertaking transactions in stocks and shares, bonds, foreign exchange currencies, options or futures with traders at commercial banks, investment banks and large institutional investors.

Further information

The Government Economics Service   www.ges.gov.uk

The Institute of Economic Affairs   www.iea.org.uk

The Economist (magazine)

R. Dransfield *Key Ideas in Economics*
(Nelson Thornes)

ENGINEERING

One definition of Engineering is that it 'involves the knowledge of the mathematical and natural sciences (biological and physical) gained by study, experience and practice that are applied with judgment and creativity to develop ways to utilize the materials and forces of nature for the benefit of mankind.' This subject introduces students to all areas of engineering and provides some of the skills and knowledge to be able work in this sector in the future.

Subject options

This subject is available at GCE A/AS level, and as a BTEC National and as one of the new Diplomas. There are also some NVQs available in this subject, but these are people who are already working in particular engineering jobs.

A/AS level

The following outline is based on the Edexcel specification:

- Unit 1: Engineering materials, processes and techniques
- Unit 2: The role of the engineer
- Unit 3: Principles of design, planning and prototyping
- Unit 4: Applied engineering systems
- Unit 5: The engineering environment
- Unit 6: Applied design, planning and prototyping.

This course is available in both AS single award (three units) and A level single award (six units). Teaching is through a combination of practical project work, case studies, talks from practising engineers and other learning from work-related context. Assessment is a mixture of internal and external examination and producing portfolios of evidence. To do well in this subject, students need a practical mind, a head for figures and some lateral thinking.

BTEC Nationals

These qualifications are aimed to give students the practical skills in computing needed by the job market in that particular sector. BTEC Nationals are available in three levels (Award, Certificate and Diploma), and are offered by Edexcel exam board:

- BTEC National Award (equivalent to one GCE A level)
- BTEC National Certificate (equivalent to two GCE A levels)
- BTEC National Diploma (equivalent to three GCE A levels).

The following subjects are available at BTEC National Award level (equivalent of one A level):

- Communications Technology
- Engineering

- Vehicle Technology
- Vehicle Technology (Motorsports).

The following subjects are available at BTEC National Certificate and Diploma level (equivalent of two or three A levels):

Aerospace Engineering	Communications Technology	Electrical/Electronic Engineering
Engineering	Manufacturing Engineering	Mechanical Engineering
Operations and Maintenance	Vehicle Technology	Vehicle Technology (Motorsports)

Assessment is by a combination of coursework, projects, case studies and examinations.

Advanced Diploma

The Diploma in Engineering will be first taught in 2008 in a way that students will experience a mixture of practical, theoretical and applied learning. You will learn about your particular subject area, but there is also a 'Functional Skills' element which includes English, Mathematics and ICT. The modules, based on the OCR specification, are as follows:

- Unit 1: Engineering business and the environment
- Unit 2: Applications of computer-aided engineering
- Unit 3: Selection and application of engineering materials
- Unit 4: Instrumentation and control engineering
- Unit 5: Maintaining engineering systems
- Unit 6: Production and manufacturing
- Unit 7: Innovative design and enterprise
- Unit 8: Mathematical techniques and applications for engineering
- Unit 9: Specific principles for engineers.

Students are continually assessed throughout the course and they have to complete an extended project and a period of work experience.

Choosing other subjects to go with Engineering

Other subjects that would go well with this one include Maths, Physics, Computing/ICT, Design and Technology, Manufacturing and Construction and the Built Environment.

Engineering at HE level

There are many different types of Engineering and this is reflected in the types of Engineering courses available at degree level. Interestingly, most universities specify A levels in Maths and Physics rather any previous Engineering qualifications, so bear this in mind when choosing your subjects.

A degree in Engineering?

Some of the types of Engineering degrees include the following:

- Civil Engineering
- Chemical Engineering
- Electronic and Electrical Engineering
- Mechanical Engineering
- Telecommunications Engineering.

Some of the courses have better links with the Engineering industry than others; investigate this before taking the plunge.

Combining Engineering with other degree subjects

Engineering goes well with a number of subjects, most notably Mathematics and Physics. A few combinations currently offered by universities include:

- Civil with Environmental Engineering
- Chemical Engineering with Biochemical Engineering
- Electronic Engineering with Computer Science
- Engineering with Business Finance
- Engineering with Business Management.

Foundation degrees and Diplomas

There are many Engineering-related Foundation degrees available and you can search for them at www.ucas.com. There are also BTEC Higher Nationals available in many different types of Engineering and you can find these listed on the websites of exam boards such as Edexcel.

Engineering and your future career

Non-graduate jobs

With an A level in Engineering, you should already be aware of the career routes open to you in Engineering and indeed you may be able to get a place on some training schemes or apprenticeships with Engineering and construction companies for instance. Non-engineering positions will still be open to you of course.

Graduate jobs directly related to Engineering

Opportunities in engineering fall into the following categories, but differ in detail and context:

- Commercial engineering and customer services
- Engineering design
- Engineering research and development

- Installation and commissioning engineering
- Information technology and management services
- Manufacturing and processing
- Process engineering, control and maintenance.

Postgraduate qualifications can be valuable if you want to specialise, but further study is only essential if you want to pursue a career in research.

Graduate jobs where Engineering could be useful

The following represent some of the other potential areas of employment.

- **Chartered management accountant:** provides financial information needed for planning and control of industrial or commercial companies, establishes and maintains financial policies and systems.
- **Management consultant:** provides advice on corporate strategy, organisational development, financial and administrative systems, human resources and information technology.
- **Production manager:** plans, co-ordinates and operates manufacturing and allied production processes to ensure most efficient use of plant, manpower and materials.
- **Systems analyst/systems developer:** investigates and analyses a client's data processing needs. Designs, tests and implements a system to meet these needs. Writes new programs or modifies existing software to run the system.
- **Technical sales engineer:** acts as a link between a company producing technical goods and services and its customers, negotiating sales, orders, price and quality in order to meet their technical and commercial requirements.

Further information

Association for Women in Science and Engineering	www.awise.org
Construction Careers Website	www.careersinconstruction.com
Institution of Mechanical Engineers	www.imeche.org

ENGLISH

Students of English can focus on language alone, literature alone or choose a course in both language and literature. Those studying English Language consider some of the following questions: What are the origins of the English Language? How has it changed over time? How is it used differently according to different situations, contexts and purposes? What makes the journalism in one newspaper different to another? What are jargon, idiom and cliché

Literature students are asked to think about, through a close examination of literary texts, a whole range of questions about life. Literature encourages us to think about such broad issues, and intersects with many other subjects such as history, psychology, philosophy, religion, art and sociology. The kinds of issues English Literature students could consider include: What is the author's view of contemporary society? What literary methods does the poet use to create a particular effect in the poem? How does Shakespeare's language differ from our own? What are the main recurring themes in this novel?

English Language and Literature allows students the opportunity to study English from both a linguistic and a literary perspective. It gives them the opportunity to study a far more varied range of texts than for a pure Literature course would and is less focused on structure, semantics and linguistics than a pure Language course would be. Some of the questions that students of this course consider include: How do language and literature link together? How is language used in particular literary genres such as poetry, prose and drama? How do I critically compare two or more pieces of literature and/or language? How is language adapted according to different audiences?

Subject options

These subjects are available at GCE A/AS level and there is also an AEA in English which is accessible to students who've taken any of the three English-related subjects.

A/AS level English Language

The outline below is based on what the majority of exam board syllabuses include. For an exact definition of the syllabus you will be studying, you should consult your school or college or even the exam board itself. Students who are finding it difficult to choose between English Language and English Literature should be aware that OCR offers a combined course in English Language and Literature, but your school or college might not be able to offer this option. *NB: AEA level in English is available to students of the course. It is offered through OCR exam board.*

Introduction to language study
Students explore a variety of texts to learn some of the characteristics of the English language including structure, stylistics, semantics and linguistics

Using language

This element of the course allows students to develop their own writing skills and compare what they have written to a series of texts.

Interacting through language

Students study how language is used in face-to-face encounters and identify the speaking and listening skills required to be an effective communicator. Includes theorists' views of face-to-face communication and linguistic analysis.

Language variation and change

How language is used in different times and settings is the focus of this part of the course and students learn how the language has developed since Early Modern times to the present day. Students are also taught how contemporary English is used differently in different geographical locations.

A/AS level English Literature

Students read a range of literary texts in different genres, but syllabuses will include the following elements:

Prose/Fiction

Most syllabuses also include a stipulation that students gain a knowledge of modern and older fiction. Some exam boards make the distinction between pre- and post-war writing (i.e. before and after 1914). Popular texts for study include: Charlotte Brontë's *Jane Eyre;* Bram Stoker's *Dracula;* Harper Lee's *To Kill a Mocking Bird;* John Steinbeck's *Of Mice and Men;* Thomas Hardy's *Tess of the D'Urbervilles;* Joseph Conrad's *Heart of Darkness* and many others.

English has a rich history of poetry, therefore exam boards have a lot to choose from. Again, choices try and reflect both modern and older poets and set texts can include: some of Chaucer's *Canterbury Tales* and Shakespeare's sonnets; and selected poems from the following writers:

- Sylvia Plath
- Seamus Heaney
- T. S. Eliot
- Tony Harris
- Anne Stevenson
- William Blake
- John Keats
- W. B. Yeats
- Tony Harrison

…as well as many others.

A/AS level English Language and Literature

The following outline is based on the OCR specification.

Linking language and literature

This unit requires students to compare literary texts with a piece of non-literary language such as a transcript of speech. In this way, students learn how different meanings are created by different literary and linguistic forms.

Language in Literature: poetry and prose

Students study various texts of poetry and prose, usually in preparation to a final examination where they have to give a close textual comment, using both literary and linguistic analysis.

Styles of writing

Students write original pieces covering both literary and non-literary styles and also provide a commentary on their own writing based on the insights gained from both literary and linguistic techniques.

Language in literature: drama

Different dramatic texts are studied usually including both Shakespeare and more contemporary plays. In the exam, students have to comment on a particular passage of text and relate it to the whole piece from both a literary and linguistic perspective. Popular texts include: *The Tempest; As You Like it; Hamlet; King Lear; Waiting for Godot; A Streetcar Named Desire.*

Issues in language and literature

This module focuses on how language and literature can be used and interpreted according to different social and political agendas. For the OCR syllabus, for instance, students can choose to focus on the 'the language of persuasion', 'language and identities' and 'language and gender'.

Genre studies

Most syllabuses have a synoptic module where students link together all they have learned on the course so far and, during an examination, are required to answer questions on unseen pieces of text and/or literature.

Advanced Extension Award

The AEA in English consists of a single three-hour examination in which students have to answer two questions from a choice of up to six. The AEA is designed to be accessible to candidates from any of the three English A levels: Literature, Language and Literature and Language. The questions will be based on a range of diverse, unseen reading material which will be centred around a given theme, topic or period. It will typically comprise the following elements:

- Unfamiliar primary texts from different genres and periods, literary and non-literary, drawn from spoken and written language, and selected to facilitate comparisons and connections.
- Some secondary texts linked to the primary reading material by, for example, authorship, context, or specific commentary, and which raise issues of literary or linguistic debate relevant to the interpretation of the primary texts.

- • Other secondary materials which demonstrate a range of critical views, theoretical positions and analytical approaches.

The exam is marked externally and students achieve either a Merit or Distinction. Students failing to earn a Merit will receive an 'ungraded' classification.

How are A/AS levels in English-related subjects taught and assessed?

Teaching is a combination of close textual analysis in classes and group discussions about particular themes. Students are also expected to do lots of reading outside of the classroom to support their learning. There will also be lots of essay writing throughout the course. Assessment is via a combination of coursework, closed examinations and 'open book' examinations. Again, as with many other subjects, the AS can be taken as a stand alone subject or taken as 50 per cent of the assessment value towards the final A2 mark.

Choosing other subjects to go with English

It's common to see students combine this subject with other arts and humanities subjects such as History, a foreign language, or Geography. Certainly, the kind of skills used in these subjects would reinforce and complement the ones developed in the study of language and literature. However, this subject would also provide a good contrast for students who are also studying more science-based subjects.

English at HE level

At degree level, there are many courses that include language and literature and many where it's possible to study literature and language as single subjects. To get a place on one of these degree courses you would need a good A level grade in at least one of the following: English Language and Literature, English Literature, or English Language.

A degree in English?

Degrees in English usually have core components such as 'Anglo-Saxon literature' or 'the English language' and students are also given the flexibility to add a few modules of their choice to complete the degree. Specialist options might include 'the literature of James Joyce' or 'Semantics', for instance. Some degree courses have a foreign language and literature element so knowledge of a foreign language could be a help.

Combining English with other subjects at degree level

English Literature and Language is already a joint subject so it's not usual to study anything additionally. However, it's very common to see English Language or Literature combined with subjects such as History, Philosophy, a modern foreign language, Sociology and Music.

Foundation degrees and Diplomas

BTEC Higher Nationals and Foundation degrees in English Language and Literature are still pretty uncommon. They do exist, however, in related areas and in vocational areas where the knowledge and study of English is useful such as media and communications; journalism; advertising; publishing and business with English as a foreign language.

English and your future career

Non-graduate jobs

Many employers requiring A levels or equivalents do not really mind which subjects applicants have. In that sense, English is as good as choice as any as it gives students all round critical thinking, empathy and analytical skills. Furthermore, there may be some non-graduate areas of work where English is still more useful than some others because you will have developed strong skills in both written and oral communication. Jobs where these skills are especially useful include:

- marketing or sales assistants
- jobs requiring a lot of communication or telephone work
- trainee news reporter
- library assistant
- tour guide.

Graduate jobs: directly related to English

If you wish to use your degree directly there are several employment areas where a degree in English is directly relevant. Some of the most popular jobs are listed below. Further training is needed in some cases.

- **English as a foreign language teacher/English as a second language teacher:** teaching English to foreign students in either the UK or overseas.
- **HE Lecturer in English Language and Literature:** teaching university students about literature. After your degree, you would generally need an MA and a PhD to get a lectureship.
- **Primary school teacher and Secondary school teacher:** opportunities exist in secondary and primary schools as well as in independent schools, sixth form colleges and in further or Higher Education.

Graduate jobs where English could be useful

There are careers which traditionally attract English graduates more than others and which can make use of many of the skills that are acquired through studying the subject.

- **Advertising account executive:** co-ordinates, plans and organises advertising campaigns in consultation with clients.
- **Advertising copywriter:** writes original advertising copy to promote and sell products or services in the press, on television and radio or on posters.

- **Charity officer:** involves a wide range of responsibilities including aspects of marketing, finance, fund-raising, public relations etc. Includes organising events, managing volunteers, meeting targets, etc.
- **Commissioning editor:** monitors the progress from commissioning to production and liaises with people involved with production of material. Develops ideas and responds to market forces.
- **Marketing executive:** formulates a marketing plan for a product/service and brings it to fruition.
- **Newspaper journalist:** reports on news and other items of current interest for newspapers.
- **Programme researcher, broadcasting/film/video:** generates programme ideas, researches background material, briefs production teams and presenters.
- **Public relations officer:** projects and maintains a desirable image of an organisation and keeps the public informed of developments of general interest.
- **Television/film/video producer:** responsible for turning ideas into programmes within the allocated budget.

Further information

The National Council for the Training
of Journalists   www.nctj.com

The Society of Authors   www.societyofauthors.net

C. Baldick The Concise Dictionary of Literary
Terms (OUP, 2004)

B. Bryson, *Mother Tongue* (Penguin, 1991)

A. Gardiner, *English Language: A level Study Guide*
(Pearson, 2003)

ENVIRONMENTAL STUDIES

Environmental Studies is all about the how humans interact with their environment. Given the growing public and political concern about environmental issues, it is hardly a surprise that this subject is becoming more and more popular among students. Students learn about the scientific concepts in relation to environmentalism but also the social, political and economic aspects of managing the environment such as sustainability and conservation.

Subject options

Environmental Studies is only available at GCE A/AS level, but there are some land-based BTEC National courses which some students may find interesting. You can find details of these through the Edexcel website (www.edexcel.org.uk). From September 2009, there is also a new Environmental and Land-based Studies Diploma available.

A/AS level

The outline below is based on the new AQA specification.

Unit 1: The living environment

Why conservation is important; methods of effective conservation; national and international conservation efforts; ecology, organisms and the environment.

Unit 2: The physical environment

Atmospheric gases, water and mineral nutrients; human exploitation and the effective management of physical resources; unsustainable natural resources.

Unit 3: Energy resources and environmental pollution

Energy supply shortage and possible solutions; pollutants; minimising the release of toxic materials.

Unit 4: Biological resources and sustainability

Human population growth and its demands on the environment; food production and forestry systems; human lifestyles and sustainability.

AS students complete units one and two; A2 candidates complete units one to four. Assessment is by written paper under examination conditions.

Advanced Diploma

The Advanced Diploma in Environmental and Land-based Studies This is a new qualification that will be available in some schools and colleges in England from September 2009, and will be available throughout England by 2013. The Diploma can be studied at Foundation, Higher and Advanced levels. An Extended Level Diploma will become available from 2011.

The Diploma is made up of three components:

- **Principal learning:** the main compulsory component of the Diploma, which develops hands-on knowledge, understanding and skills in the context of the environmental and land-based sector.
- **Generic learning:** compulsory learning, including functional skills in English, maths and ICT, plus the development of personal, learning and thinking skills, and the opportunity for learners to develop through work-related learning and work experience.
- **Additional or specialist learning:** an opportunity to study further environmental and land-based topics in more depth, or to broaden the range of study.

Choosing other subjects to go with Environmental Studies

Environmental Studies obviously goes very well with Geography and, to a certain extent, Biology but other subjects that are compatible include Politics, Economics and Law. Most degree courses won't specify that an A level in Environment Studies is needed, but most prefer at least a qualification in Geography.

Environment Studies at HE level

At HE level, courses in this area are usually called either Environmental Science or Environmental Studies. The former, not surprisingly, tends to have more of a scientific emphasis, whereas the latter looks in more detail at the social and political aspects. Many courses degrees emphasise the importance of integrating biology, chemistry and geography in order to understand the science of human impact on the environment and how these need to be applied within the context of social, legal and political frameworks to resolve some of the major environmental issues facing the world.

A degree in Environmental Studies?

A typical degree in this subject would have some core subjects in the first year with some options in the second and third years. Instruction takes the form of lectures, tutorials, seminars, practicals, fieldwork and research projects, all of which vary in form and content between departments. Fieldwork includes specific field project modules as well as projects on air and water quality. Most students are required to undertake final year research projects and these too may include a substantial element of fieldwork.

Combining Environmental Studies with other degree subjects

It is quite common to see this subject combined with Physics, Biology, Chemistry, Maths, Geography, Development Studies, Politics and Computer Science.

Foundation degrees and Diplomas

There are a number of environmentally-related Foundation degrees which you can search for at www.ucas.com.

Environmental Studies and your future career

Non-graduate jobs

Most jobs working in the environmental field involve further training but you may be able get some experience in environmental charities, especially if you have good administrative or secretarial skills. Your A level in this subject will have developed your skills in analysis, logical thinking and problem solving and you should always try and demonstrate these to potential employers whatever the sector.

Graduate jobs directly related to Environmental Studies

There has been an increase in the range of careers where an environmental science/studies degree is one of the required disciplines. Postgraduate qualifications may be required or could enhance your skills. Some of the related jobs include:

- **Countryside manager:** works for a local authority to manage countryside and visitor services within that area.
- **Environmental education officer:** supports, sustains and develops environmental issues within the community. May involve school visits, giving talks, leading walks, producing educational resources and developing innovative ways of promoting sustainable development.
- **Environmental manager:** implements initiatives through local authorities in the UK, e.g. sustainable development programmes, programmes for the reduction of pollution and other environmentally linked policies in their area.
- **Nature conservation officer:** responsible for the protection, management and development of wildlife habitats in a National or Country Park, private estate or other conservation site.
- **Recycling officer:** responsible for local authorities' environmental policies for waste reduction, re-use and recovery. Develops plans, implements and monitors a variety of recycling schemes.
- **Water quality scientist:** scientific analysis of water samples for the purpose of maintaining quality to set targets and standards.
- **Waste disposal officer:** works with local authorities, which are responsible for waste regulation, or with waste disposal companies in the fields of: site operations; control and monitoring of the environmental effects of waste disposal; development of new methods of managing all types of waste disposal (recycling, high temperature incineration, etc.).

Graduate jobs where a degree in Environmental Studies could be useful

- **Environmental consultant:** works on client contracts in areas such as water pollution, air and land contamination, waste management, environmental impact assessment, environmental audit, ecological management, environmental policy, etc.
- **Environmental health officer:** monitors and ensures the maintenance of standards of environmental and public health – including food and food hygiene, safety at work, housing, noise and pollution control – in accordance with the law.
- **Property and construction:** landscape architecture, town planning, cartography, geographical information systems.
- **Public health and consumer protection:** occupational and public health, health and safety inspectorates, environmental health.
- **Secondary school teacher:** geography, science, depending on core subjects within first degree.
- **Toxicologist:** carries out scientific identification and studies effects of harmful chemicals, biological materials and radiation on living systems and the environment to see how they can be avoided or minimised.
- **Transportation planner:** identifies need for transport infrastructure, manages travel demand and changes people's travel behaviour in line with government guidelines, e.g. reducing car use and promoting walking, cycling and public transport.

Further information

Department for Environment, Food
and Rural Affairs (DEFRA)   www.defra.gov.uk

The Environment Agency   www.environment-agency.gov.uk

K. Byrne, *Environmental Science*
(Nelson Thornes, 2001)

FILM STUDIES

As a student of Film Studies you will broaden and deepen both your knowledge and enjoyment of films. The emphasis of the course is on how films convey meanings in different ways and how they are subject to the social, cultural, political and economic forces of the time at which they were created. As well as analysing different genres of films, students will compare Hollywood and British films and analyse specific cinematic techniques. How the film and cinema industry operates is also part of this course.

Subject options

At the time of writing, Film Studies is available at GCE A/AS level and the only exam board to offer this course is WJEC. However, the CCEA exam board offers an A/AS level in Moving Image Arts which is a much more technical and practical course.

Also, from September 2008, a new Advanced Diploma in Creative and Media will be available for study. Please see page 147 for further details.

A/AS level

Unit 1: Exploring film form
This unit focuses on analysing the form and style of certain types of films. The relationship between form and how an audience interprets a film is also important part of this.

Unit 2: British and American film
In this unit, students focus on topics in UK and US film and also complete a comparative study.

Unit 3: Film research and creative projects
Students complete a film-related research project and a creative project.

Unit 4: Varieties of film experience: issues and debates
Students learn about world cinema, spectatorship and have the opportunity to complete an in-depth critical study of a single film.

AS students complete units one and two; A2 students complete all four units. Assessment is a mixture of closed examinations and coursework.

Choosing other subjects to go with Film Studies

Subjects that complement this one include Media Studies, English Literature, Communication Studies, a Modern Foreign Language, Sociology and History. Always ensure that there isn't too much of an overlap between your subjects because exam boards may not permit the combination and universities may not recognise your UCAS points tally!

Film Studies at HE level

There are many film courses at a higher level. Some are very academic or theoretical, others are more practical or vocational in their approach. You have to decide which type of course appeals to you more. There are also many related courses in Media Studies or Media Arts and studying film would constitute a large part of that.

A degree in Film Studies?

The breadth of your studies will be much greater at degree level than at A levels. Usually there are some core modules in the first year with some flexibility of choice of modules in years two and three. Some typical modules of a degree in Film Studies might include:

- Art and film
- Avant garde
- Border crossings in American cinema
- British cinema from the 1950s
- Cinema in 1920s Berlin, Paris and Moscow
- European cinema
- Film style, interpretation and evaluation
- Introduction to narrative cinema
- Sound and cinema
- The documentary film
- Topics in American cinema.

Combining Film Studies with other degree subjects

Subjects that are often combined with Film Studies include English Literature, a modern language, Contemporary Arts, Drama, History and Politics.

Foundation degrees and Diplomas

There are many different Foundation degrees available in specific areas of media, but none specifically in film studies alone. You can search for them at www.ucas.com. There are also a number of BTEC Higher Nationals in media-related subjects.

Film Studies and your future career

Non-graduate jobs

An A level in Film Studies will give you good skills and an insight into the film industry as well as the academic aspects of film. Getting into the film business as a career is notoriously difficult and you have to be prepared to make contacts and often work on an unpaid basis to build experience until you get your first break. Non-media careers are still open to you of course.

Graduate jobs directly related to Film Studies

Many students on these courses are interested in gaining employment in all aspects of the media industry. Careers in the media, however, are highly sought after and competition is likely to be fierce.

- **Broadcast assistant, radio:** assists with production and presentation of programmes for local and national radio stations.
- **Broadcasting presenter:** fronts the programme, specific responsibilities vary depending on the programme.
- **Journalism:** reports on news and other areas of interests for newspapers, periodicals, radio and TV.
- **Multimedia programmer:** researches, develops and produces materials for new media based company activities.
- **Programme researcher, broadcasting/film/video:** acts as an assistant producer with responsibility for conception and implementation of a programme.
- **Radio producer:** responsible for initiating ideas, selling these to commissioning editors and managing the technical and creative team to produce the final programme.
- **Television/film/video producer:** undertakes the artistic interpretation of materials and directs the production of shows/films.
- **Television production assistant:** provides organisational and secretarial services for programme director.

Graduate jobs where film studies could be useful

- **Advertising account executive:** takes overall responsibility for co-ordination, planning and organisation of advertising campaigns.
- **Editorial assistant:** assists editorial staff in the commissioning, planning and production of books, journals and magazines.
- **Event organiser:** identifies potential business, researches, writes, plans and runs all types of conferences on behalf of a client or own organisation.
- **Information officer/manager:** ensures effective communication of information relating to a particular field of interest.
- **Market research executive:** undertakes systematic research to determine the potential market for a product or service.
- **Public relations account executive:** PR agencies work for their clients in presenting their image to the public. They decide on strategies to be used and which media would be the most effective.

Further information

The British Film Institute   www.bfi.org.uk/education

Skillset   www.skillset.org; www.skillsformedia.com

T. O'Sullivan, B. Dutton and P. Rayner
Studying the Media (Hodder Arnold, 2003)

GENERAL STUDIES

General Studies is a bit different from most subjects in that it is not the study of a single discipline; rather it seeks to broaden students' minds by teaching aspects from various different disciplines and areas of life. As well as learning about issues and acquiring knowledge of contemporary and historic matters, one of the aims of the course is to develop in students the skills of critical and logical thinking so that they can form their own opinions about things in the world.

Subject options

This subject is available as GCE A/AS level and is offered by Edexcel, OCR and AQA exam boards. The outline below is based on what the majority of exam board syllabuses include, but there is often some variation in the title of modules. For an exact definition of the syllabus you will be studying, you should consult your school or college or even the exam board itself. Some of the themes studied include:

- Culture, morality, arts and humanities
- Critical thinking and analytical skills
- Science, mathematics and technology
- Society, politics and the economy.

How is A/AS level General Studies taught and assessed?

A level candidates usually have about four compulsory units and, AS candidates usually have two compulsory options. Assessment is usually by written exams. You don't need GCSE General Studies to study this subject.

Choosing other subjects to go with General Studies

NB: Some universities do not recognise General Studies as a qualifying subject – General Studies should be in addition to your 'regular' subjects, not instead of. In this sense any other subjects may added to the General Studies course.

General Studies at HE level

There are no degree programmes in General Studies.

Foundation degrees and Diplomas

There are no Foundation degrees and Diplomas in this subject.

General Studies and your future career

There are no specific jobs related to this subject but employers appreciate people who have a broad base of knowledge and who can think for themselves. General Studies aims to equip students with both of these things. However, like many universities, many employers don't recognise General Studies as a 'legitimate' A level subject.

GEOGRAPHY

Students of Geography learn about the environment in which we live and the way humans interact in that environment. On the one hand students learn about the physical aspects of the earth (physical geography) and on the other they learn about humans use and adapt to their surrounds (human/ urban geography) as well as the interaction between the two. Geography is a truly interdisciplinary subject calling on and developing kills in research, numeracy, spatial awareness, as well as critical and analytical thinking. Some of the most political issues are often considered by A level geographers including decisions to build new motorways or runways; the effects of natural disasters and floods; immigration; food shortage and famine as well as many other topics.

Subject options

Geography is available at GCE A/AS level and it's available for study as an Advanced Extension Award (AEA). You might also be interested in the A/AS level in World Development offered by WJEC.

A/AS level

Most of the exam boards offer courses with some or more of the following elements. For an exact definition of the AS and A2 syllabus you will be studying, you should consult your school, college or the exam board itself.

Core concepts in Physical Geography:

- Water on land
- Climatic hazards and change
- Energy and life.

Core concepts in Human Geography:

- Population dynamics
- Settlement processes and patterns
- Economic activity.

Challenge and change in the Natural Environment:

- Coasts – processes and problems
- Geomorphological processes and hazards (the shaping of the earth's surfaces by environmental forces)
- Cold environments and human activity
- Sustainability.

Advanced Extension Award

AEAs draw up on all the different elements that students have learned throughout their A2 course to candidates' abilities to:

- Apply and communicate effectively their knowledge of Geography
- Use the skills of critical analysis, evaluation and synthesis
- Reach clear, logical and coherent judgements.

It is aimed at candidates who will in all likelihood gain a Grade A at GCE level. Examination is by written paper and is externally assessed. AEA Geography is offered by WJEC exam board on behalf of all the examining boards in the UK.

How is A/AS level Geography taught and assessed?

Like most subjects there is an element of learning from textbooks and classroom note-taking. However, students of this subject will work with maps, statistical data, weather reports, case studies, they will carry out surveys and create questionnaires, watch videos. They will also carry out fieldwork and may visit locations of geographical interest. To do well at this subject, students need to be good all-rounders with the ability to think and analyse different types of data. AS candidates complete 50 per cent of the modules.

Choosing other subjects to go with Geography

Geography can be very scientific at one end of the spectrum and very social at the other. In this sense, it can go very well with a wide range of subjects. Common accompaniments to the subject include Environmental Science, Biology, History, Mathematics, Physics and Chemistry. If you want to study Geography at Higher Education level, then it could affect your choice of post-16 subjects because some degree courses are very science-based while others are much more humanities-based.

Geography at HE level

Geography at degree level can be offered as a science subject (BSc) or an arts subject (BA), or both. This largely depends on the outlook of the department and the emphasis of a particular course. Most institutions will ask for A level Geography to get a place, but there may be some exceptions to this.

A degree in Geography?

A BSc Geography tends to focus more on physical geography and the BA Geography tends to focus more on Human Geography. Some universities offer some flexibility so that students can choose options from both degree programmes. Despite this, there is usually some core courses (usually in the first year at least) and thereafter some choice about the remaining modules to be taken. Fieldwork is also an important part of a degree in Geography and many institutions run fieldwork trips in Britain and abroad. Some of the modules that could form part of a typical degree programme in Geography include the following:

- Geography, society and development
- Global environmental change
- Global environmental issues
- Global environmental problems and policies
- Historical geographies of urbanism
- Hydrology
- Methods in geographical analysis
- Natural hazards
- Readings in geography
- The natural environment
- Tropical forests in a changing environment.

Combining Geography with other degree subjects

If allowed by the institution, Geography can be combined with many other degree subjects including a modern foreign language, Environmental Science, History, Computer Science, Development Studies, English and Biology, as well as many others.

Foundation degrees and Diplomas

There are no Foundation degrees specifically in Geography, but there are some in environmentally related topics. Similarly, there are no BTEC Higher Nationals in Geography but there are some in Land- and environmentally related studies.

Geography and your future career

Non-graduate jobs

You will gain lots of varied skills from A level Geography which you could apply to lots of different areas of work. If you want to work in a Geography-related area though, you would probably have to study the subject at a degree-level first.

Graduate jobs directly related to a degree in Geography

Some of the following jobs require further training or study and relevant practical experience.

- **Cartographer:** evaluates sets of geographical data and presents it in the form of diagrams, charts and spreadsheets as well as conventional maps.
- **Distribution/logistics manager:** manages the supply, movement and storage of goods and materials. You would plan, organise and co-ordinate the flow and storage of materials through the whole supply chain process from manufacturer to customer.
- **Environmental consultant:** works in areas such as air and land contamination, water pollution, noise and vibration measurement, waste management, environmental policy and ecological/land management.

- **Geographical information systems manager:** manages a team of IT professionals who use computer-based systems to handle geographical information.
- **Remote sensing scientist:** processes aerial photographs and satellite images by computer in order to fit them to maps or to enhance specific features of interest and to assess their significance.
- **Secondary school teacher:** develops schemes of work and plans lessons in line with national objectives. As a secondary school teacher you must also keep up to date with developments in your subject area and with new resources and methods.
- **Town planner:** directs or undertakes the planning of land use. This involves taking into account the views of interested parties in order to find a balance between the conflicting demands of housing, industrial development, agriculture, recreation, transport network, the environment, etc.
- **Transportation planner:** identifies the need for a transport infrastructure, devises transport strategies in line with government guidelines, e.g. reducing car use and promoting walking, cycling and public transport. Statistical analysis is used to forecast developments.

Graduate jobs where a degree in Geography could be useful

The following represent some common areas of employment into which geographers enter.

- **Local government administrator:** responds to the needs of individual departments, sometimes as a specialist in administration, finance or personnel. You would assist in the formulation of policies and procedures and co-ordinate their implementation.
- **Nature conservation officer:** protects, manages and enhances wildlife habitats. Your work may include promoting and implementing local biodiversity action plans through negotiation with planners and developers, conservation tasks, visitor liaison or educational and interpretative work.
- **Tourism officer:** develops and promotes tourism in order to attract visitors and to produce significant economic benefits for a particular region or site.
- **Urban general practice surveyor:** values, manages and markets residential and commercial property and acts as an agent for clients in the purchase, leasing or sale of property.

Further information

The Association of Geographic Information   www.agi.org.uk

The Royal Geographical Society   www.rgs.org

A. Barker, D. Redfern and M. Skinner, *Advanced Geography* (Philip Allan, 2006)

GEOLOGY

Students of Geology will learn all about the characteristics of the Earth's surface including rocks and soil as well as the rocks and minerals that make up the earth's crust, mantle and core. Geology is not fascinating just because students learn about the physical properties of the earth, but because this subject gives an insight into the origins of the planet and how it has changed over time. It is also an important discipline because it teaches us much about the causes of natural disasters such as volcanoes, earthquakes and tsunami.

Subject options

The exam boards offers A/AS level Geology: OCR and WJEC.

A/AS level

The outline below is based on the OCR exam board.

Unit 1: Global tectonics and geological structures
The Structure of the earth; earthquakes; global tectonics; geological structures.

Unit 2: The rock cycle – processes and products
The rock cycle (the study of igneous, sedimentary and metamorphic rocks); sedimentary processes and products; igneous processes and products; metamorphic processes and products.

Unit 3: Practical skills in geology 1
Students complete a practical task, possibly as fieldwork.

Unit 4: Environmental geology
Water supply; energy resources; metallic mineral deposits; engineering geology.

Unit 5: Evolution of life, earth and climate
Formation of fossils; morphology and organisms; fossil evidence; climate change; dating methods and interpreting geological maps.

Unit 6: Practical skills in geology 2
Students complete a practical task, possibly as fieldwork.

How is A/AS level Geology taught and assessed?

Geology is a science subject, so practical and lab work is an important element. It is suitable for candidates looking for a broad base in science at Advanced level and also supports subjects such as Geography – the ideas extend GCSE Science and are complementary to AS/Advanced GCE Geography. No previous knowledge of geology is required, but students should have taken Science Intermediate level. Assessment is via written exams, fieldwork and coursework. AS students complete units one to three; A2 students complete all six.

Choosing other subjects to go with Geology

Other subjects that would go well with geology at AS or Advanced GCE are Biology, Chemistry, Geography and Physics. Candidates concentrating on arts, humanities or modern language subjects may wish to take geology to AS level to broaden studies by continuing to take a science subject.

Geology at HE level

If you want to study Geology at a higher level you will probably need post-16 qualifications from the following subjects: Physics, Chemistry, Biology, Geology, Geography and Environmental Science.

A degree in Geology?

Some of the Geology-related degree programmes on offer include:

- Computational Geoscience
- Environmental Geoscience
- Geology
- Geology and Geophysics
- Geophysics.

Combining Geology with other degree subjects

Subjects that go well with Geology include Physics, Biology, Computer Science, Geography, Archaeology and Environmental Science. There will be variations in which combinations universities are prepared to offer.

Foundation degrees and Diplomas

There are no Foundation degrees available in Geology but there are BTEC Higher Nationals available in Land and Environment which has some overlap with Geology.

Geology and your future career

Non-graduate jobs

You will gain lots of varied skills from Geology which you could apply to lots of different areas of work. These skills include numeracy, analytical ability, good judgement and IT skills. If you want to work in a Geology-related area though, you would probably have to study the subject at a degree level first.

Graduate jobs directly related to Geology

- **Engineering geologist:** assesses the impact of ground conditions on development schemes such as tunnels, buildings, pipelines, docks, bridges and other structures.
- **Geoscientist:** locates and proves the existence of oil, gas, minerals and water reserves, estimating the extent and quality of the find.
- **Hydro geologist:** identifies the type, distribution and structure of rock strata and their impact on the movement and accumulation of groundwater.
- **Minerals surveyor:** assists in the planning of mineral workings, ensuring the stability of mine sites and advising on the future restoration or redevelopment of exhausted sites.
- **Mudlogger:** based on an oil drilling rig, collecting and monitoring information and samples from drilling operations to report back to drilling teams and oil companies.
- **Seismic interpreter:** interprets geophysical and geological data to produce maps of structures and to evaluate the prospect of recovering hydrocarbons.
- **Wellsite geologist:** supervises the logging of an oil or gas well, co-ordinates the collection and interpretation of well data and communicates the results to management and other colleagues.

Graduate jobs where a degree in Geology could be useful

The following examples illustrate some areas of work that can give you the opportunity to use the skills and knowledge gained from a Geology degree.

- **Geographical information systems manager:** integrates a variety of data into a relational database which gives the user the power to integrate spatial data into a topographical framework.
- **Hydrologist:** analyses water flow through pipes and channels for the engineering and control of water. The focus of the work is on surface water and can include estimating yields of water and investigating its quality.
- **Waste disposal officer:** tasks could include managing a landfill site, organising household waste collection systems including tendering for contracts and researching and implementing methods of toxic waste disposal.

Further information

Earthworks	www.earthworks-jobs.com
Geological Society	www.geolsoc.org.uk
Jobsite for Geologists	www.geologyshop.co.uk/jobs

GOVERNMENT AND POLITICS

Students of this subject will learn about many different aspects of Government and Politics. Some of the questions that they may consider include:

- How have political systems changed over time?
- How do political structures and voting systems work?
- What is democracy and how does that concept differ according to different contexts and periods of history?
- What are the responsibilities of government and how do they exert their power?
- What are some of the differences between the US and UK political systems?

Issues such as human rights, justice, war and peace may also be studied.

Subject options

This subject is available at GCE A/AS level and is offered by OCR and AQA. For an exact definition of the AS and A2 syllabus you will be studying, you should consult your school, college or the exam board itself. Some common elements of an A level course in Government and Politics include the following, although the title of modules may vary among the different exam boards:

- People and politics
- Governing in the UK
- The changing UK system; participation and voting behaviour
- UK political issues; introducing political ideologies; representation in the USA; introducing international politics
- The EU and European issues; other ideological traditions; governing the USA; issues in international politics
- Policy-making in the UK; ideological development in the UK; international politics in the UK.

AS candidates study and are assessed on 50 per cent of the available modules; A2 candidates usually study all, or elements of all, of them.

How is A/AS level Government and Politics taught and assessed?

Teaching is mainly by classroom and textbook work but students may also look at news reports, political party manifestos and many other politically related texts. Sometimes schools and colleges invite speakers to come and talk to students or visit political organisations. Assessment is mainly by written exams.

Choosing other subjects to go with Government and Politics

This subject goes well with many others including English, History, Law, Business, Economics, Sociology and a few others.

Government and Politics at HE level

There isn't usually a requirement for Government and Politics A level for entry onto degree courses. Institutions usually ask for three good grades but some may prefer subjects in the arts and humanities.

A degree in Government and Politics?

Most university degrees are called BA Politics and like many courses usually have some core elements in the first year with some optional modules to make up the remainder of the second and third years. For many courses, optional courses may include:

- Advanced policy analysis
- Comparative politics of Western Europe
- Environmental policy.
- European Union
- Fascism
- History of political thought
- Islam and the Middle East
- Karl Marx
- Politics of development
- Political leadership in the 20th Century.

Some courses may also involve some fieldwork where students spend some time at political organisations such as a political party or a pressure group or may go abroad to organisations such as the European Parliament, NATO or the European Commission.

Combining Government and Politics with other degree subjects

Politics goes well with subjects such as Law, Economics, History, Philosophy, Sociology and Modern Languages.

Foundation degrees and Diplomas

There are some Politics-related Foundation degrees but none solely focusing on the subject.

Politics and your future career

Non-graduate jobs

There are a few jobs that students could go into that are related to Government and Politics straight after a Level 3 qualification. These include junior positions in the

Civil Service or in local government. Additionally, the skills students gain from the course are transferable to many different areas of work.

Graduate jobs directly related to Government and Politics

There are very few careers where a first degree in politics is essential, or directly relevant. There are some jobs which are closely related to a politics degree but they may also require relevant experience or further training. The following are most closely related to Politics:

- **Charity fundraiser and Charity officer:** entry for both types of work may initially have to be on a voluntary basis.
- **Political party research officer:** employed in a variety of settings, including Higher Education, political parties and independent agencies. Includes working for members of Parliament and members of European Parliament.
- **Public affairs consultant (lobbyist):** represents the clients' case to those in government who make decisions that affect them. The client may be a large company, a trade association, a pressure group or a local authority.
- **Political party agent:** responsible for press coverage, publicity and liaison between the local party and the Member of Parliament.

Graduate jobs where a degree in Government and Politics could be useful

- **Civil Service fast streamer:** responds to the needs of individual departments, sometimes as a specialist in administration, finance, or personnel. Assists in the formulation of policies and procedures and co-ordinates their implementation.
- **Journalist:** responsible for gathering news and reporting work in both written and broadcast media. This involves developing contacts, interviewing people, attending press conferences and producing copy to a deadline.
- **Personnel officer:** responsible for advising on all policies relating to the use of human resources. The organisation and implementation of policies for workforce planning, recruitment, training, terms and conditions of employment and benefits.
- **Police officer:** first and foremost graduates should be committed to the role of a police officer. However, those with potential and continued high performance may be fast-tracked for promotion.
- **Public relations account executive:** responsible for the transmission of positive information to particular audiences whose attitudes require influencing, using press and media liaison, company newspapers and journals.
- **Social researcher:** designs, formulates and carries out social research in a variety of settings including central and local government, independent research institutions and Trades Unions. This would only be appropriate if your degree scheme contains a component of research methodology.
- **Solicitor:** advises individuals and organisations on legal problems; prepares wills, contracts and other legal documents; researches and advises on points of law.

Further information

Civil Service Careers Page

www.civilservice.gov.uk/careers

UK Parliament Homepage

www.parliament.uk

Read daily newspapers, especially
the broadsheets

HEALTH AND SOCIAL CARE (APPLIED)

This is one of the new applied A levels recently introduced. The emphasis of this course is very much on the vocational contexts of Health and Social Care. Furthermore, this course provides a pathway for candidates wishing to progress to Higher Education courses in the area of Health and Social Care as well as providing a useful introduction to employment in the sector. What are the most effective ways of caring for particular age groups? What is the role of exercise in the maintenance of good health? What are the career paths available in the Health and Social Care field? These are just some of the questions that students of this course consider.

Subject options

This course is available at GCE A/AS level but there is a BTEC National qualification called Health and Care also available.

Some students may also be interested in the new Advanced Diploma in Society, Health and Development, which is available from September 2008.

A/AS level

The outline below is based on what the main exam board syllabuses include. For an exact definition of the GCE syllabus you will be studying, you should consult your school or college or even the exam board itself.

Courses generally include a mixture of compulsory units and some optional ones from a range of possible choices. The following units give an outline of the main areas covered:

Effective caring	Promoting good health
Caring for young people	Caring for older people
Complementary therapies	Caring for people with disabilities
Anatomy and physiology in practice	Working in health and social care
Child and human development	Health, illness and disease
Nutrition	Effective communication
Health and safety in care settings	Diagnosis and treatment

This subject is taught by a mixture of tutor-led activities, independent research and reading and practical work. The important thing is that the context for this subject is very much work-related. Students might visit Health and Social Care environments and they may have speakers in to talk about their work or current issues. Assessment is by a mixture of internal examination of prepared portfolios of work and by written exam marked by the exam board. Students don't need to have studied this subject previously but do need to demonstrate an interest in the area. At AS GCE level, single (three units) and double (six units) awards are available. At GCE level, single (six units) and double (12 units) awards are available.

BTEC Nationals

BTEC Nationals in Health and Care are available in three levels (Award, Certificate and Diploma), and are offered by Edexcel exam board:

Topics available at BTEC National Award level (equivalent of one A level):

- Children's Care, Learning and Development
- Health and Social Care.

Topics available at BTEC National Certificate and Diploma level (equivalent of two or three A levels):

- Children's Care, Learning and Development
- Health and Social Care
- Health and Social Care (Social Care)
- Health and Social Care (Health Sciences)
- Health and Social Care (Health Studies).

Assessment for this course is by completion of a portfolio of evidence, but students must spend a certain period of working in a relevant setting.

Advanced Diploma

An overview of the content of the Diploma in Society, Health and Development is geiven below

Work experience. With a Diploma you'll get to learn all about your chosen subject through a range of core and optional elements. You'll also get at least 10 days' work experience. This is a great way to use the skills you have learn in the classroom and experience what work is like from the inside.

For example, you might work in a youth club or in an early years' nursery. Or if you're interested in social work, you might assist carers in a residential home.

Student Project. You will also be required to complete a project to demonstrate the skills and knowledge you have acquired. You can choose your own project, for example, a student working in a youth club might consider ways of redesigning the common room. You could look at ways to make it more appealing and accessible for people of all kinds of backgrounds and abilities.

Assessment

Compulsory elements. At Foundation level, you will study eight topics to give you a broad understanding of the sector and the way it works. Examples include the health, wellbeing and lifestyle of individuals and an introduction to partnership working, which looks at the ways in which agencies work together to provide services.

Higher-level students are introduced to the work of the different professions in more detail. For example, you may look at patient care or patterns of offending behaviour and the factors that can lead to this.

Along with core elements, you'll also learn how to work with other people and express yourself confidently in a work environment. And at the end, you'll complete a final Student Project to show that you can apply the skills you've learnt in a work context.

Choosing other subjects to go with Health and Social Care

This subject could be combined with many subjects but ones that seem most compatible include Sociology and Social Policy, Government and Politics, Physical Education and Business Studies. Students may also be interested in the BTEC National courses in Public Services.

Health and Social Care at HE level

Students may opt for courses such as Sociology or Social Policy; others may be interested in courses such as Health Studies or Health Economics. Each course is different and may require specific subjects at GCE level for you to be able to gain a place. A course such as Health Economics would probably require an Economics background rather than one in Health and Social Care, for instance.

A degree in Health and Social Care?

There are many different options at university level and the whole area of Health and Social Care is usually broken down into specific areas such as the following:

- Community Health and Nursing Studies
- Community and Youth Studies
- Health Studies
- Human Services
- Nursing Studies
- Primary Care
- Social Work.

Often these courses aim to give you a professional qualification in a particular area (e.g. social work) or are for currently experienced professionals who want to earn a degree. If you want a more academic course, you could want to consider degrees such as Social Policy, Health Care Policy, Sociology and others of a similar nature.

Combining a degree in Health and Social Care with other subjects

Combinations depend on the flexibility of the school you're studying at and your particular range of interests. But this degree subject may be combined well with other disciplines including Sociology, Social Policy, Politics, Public Sector Administration, Biology and Management.

Foundation degrees and Diplomas

There are many options for Foundation degrees in this area. In fact, there is much more choice at this level than rather than trying to do a 'regular' degree in it. Courses in include Health and Social Care; Early Years; Health and Social Care Management. Search for courses at www.ucas.com. Edexcel also offers a BTEC Higher National Award in Health and Social Care.

Health and Social Care and your future career

Non-graduate jobs

It is possible to get trainee posts in some areas of work in Health and Social Care without first getting a degree. These include jobs as care assistants, some areas of nursing and social care. It's also possible to get administrative positions in these environments (e.g. in the NHS or Social Services).

Graduate jobs directly related to Health and Social Care

If you want to be a doctor, then you in most instances you would need all three Science subjects at A level, or two Sciences and A level Maths. Furthermore, for many professions allied to medicine such as being a nurse, dietician, podiatrist or occupational therapist, it would be necessary to complete a full vocational course from scratch. You would need to check entry requirements and funding. Other options closely related to Health and Social Care also often require some further postgraduate training – see some examples below.

- **Lifestyle consultant:** provides physical fitness instruction and prescription of exercise/fitness programmes for individuals.
- **Health promotion specialist:** promotes awareness of health issues to individuals and the community.
- **Health Service manager:** responsible for the provision and commissioning of local healthcare, through the management of hospital, general practitioner and community health services. The National Health Service (NHS) offers graduate training schemes for these roles.
- **Nutritional therapist:** advises clients on how to improve overall health and wellbeing by assessing needs, problems, diet and lifestyle, and recommending changes.

- **Physiotherapist:** treats a range of health problems through massage, movement, exercise and technology. Although qualified status requires a further degree, posts as physiotherapy assistants are available, providing valuable experience.
- **Social worker:** aims to provide a service to individuals and families facing problems which they are unable to manage alone. Entry involves gaining work experience and a postgraduate course.

Graduate jobs where a degree in Health and Social Care could be useful

- **Charity officer:** the size of the organisation determines the responsibilities of this role. Besides administrative tasks, the position may include fund raising, policy, public relations and education. Relevant experience may be necessary, either voluntary or paid.
- **Civil Service administrator, mainstream entry:** UK Home Civil Service departments employ administrators in a variety of roles, but tasks may include: organising services and resources, strategic planning, implementing policies, research and report writing.
- **Counsellor:** helps people in coping with problems, decisions, transitions and crises. Usually needs voluntary and life experience. An accredited counselling qualification is often necessary.
- **Further Education lecturer:** delivering specific modules on, for example, relevant vocational training courses within post-compulsory education. Professional health qualifications could enhance your chances.
- **Local government administrator:** responds to the administrative needs of individual departments. Assists in the formulation of policies and procedures.
- **Sales executive, medical:** represents pharmaceutical companies to general practitioners, retail pharmacists and hospital doctors.
- **Sports administrator:** the role varies depending on the organisation, but may include organising events, training sessions or conferences; marketing and public relations; producing literature; liaising with other agencies; financial and business administration.

Further information

Jobs in community care   www.communitycare.co.uk

NHS Careers   www.nhscareers.nhs.uk

UK Civil Service Careers   www.civilservice.gov.uk/careers

HISTORY

History is still seen as an academically sound subject, not least because it develops lots of useful skills: the ability to critically evaluate written information, weighing up evidence, empathy are just some of the qualities history students learn to demonstrate. The study of history is not just learning about the past it's about thinking about how we view the past from today's perspective. The kinds of questions that students may consider include:

- What has been the global effect of the September 11 disaster?
- What are the ramifications of the reigns of prominent politicians and monarchs?
- What were the circumstances that led to the outbreak of World Wars I and II?
- How reliable is certain types of historical evidence?
- Why did Henry VIII split from the Catholic Church in Rome?

Subject options

For an exact definition of the AS and A2 syllabus you will be studying, you should consult your school, college or the exam board itself. The main variations in History are in terms of the particular period that a school chooses students to study as well as sometimes the type of history studied (i.e. social, political, or religious history). *NB: This course is also offered at AEA level by the Edexcel exam board.*

A/AS level

Most courses will ensure that candidates get experience of the following:

- Significant historical events, issues or people
- A range of historical perspectives
- The diversity of society
- The history of more than one country or state
- A substantial element of English history
- Continuity and change over a particular period.

This is achieved in a variety of ways by different exam boards but a common pattern is as follows.

As part of most A level courses, students are usually asked to examine documents from a particular period that they are studying. It could be a diary entry, a newspaper report, a poem, a prose extract or any other piece of text. Candidates are then asked questions on the document.

Periods of English History

Most A level syllabuses also include a study of particular period of English History. This could be any period from 1000 to 1970. Particular courses tend to focus only on up to 150 years at a time.

Periods of European and World History

Students may also have the opportunity a period of history other than British or English history. The same applies in terms of the length of period studied but in general the periods offered for study for European or World History run from about 1000 to 1900 and nothing more recent than that.

The study of historically significant people

As well as the elements above, some courses offer the option of an in-depth study of great historical figures. These could include any of the following:

- Charlemagne
- Chamberlain
- Elizabeth I
- King John
- Lenin
- Napoleon I
- Oliver Cromwell
- Peter the Great
- Philip II
- Stalin.

The study of historical themes

As well as studying individuals, some exam boards offer the opportunity to study certain historical themes. These could include any of the following:

- Rebellion and disorder in England 1485–1603
- The Catholic Reformation in the 16th Century
- The Decline of Spain 1598–1700
- War and Society in Britain 1793–1918
- Civil Rights in the USA 1865–1980.

Independent study

In some cases, students can do some independent study on a particular period, theme or historical figure as part of assessed coursework.

Advanced Extension Award

The AEA in History, aimed at the top 10 per cent of candidates, consists of a single three-hour examination in which students have to answer questions based on information provided and with reference to their knowledge of History. The AEA allows students to:

- Effectively communicate historical knowledge and understanding
- Demonstrate in depth their understanding of historical terms and concepts
- Evaluate the significance of events, individuals, issues and societies in history
- Apply their critical thinking.

The exam is marked externally and students achieve either a Merit or Distinction. Students failing to earn a Merit will receive an 'ungraded' classification.

How is A/AS level History taught and assessed?

Class lessons may also include practice of analysing historical documents, watching relevant historical programmes and group discussions. As with subjects such as English Literature, the volume of reading and writing is high in this subject and students should be prepared for that before they embark on subject. Assessment varies from exam board: some may have final exams only; others have elements of assessed coursework, independent projects and open book examinations.

Choosing other subjects to go with History

History is often combined with other A level subjects such as English Literature, Sociology, Geography, a Modern Language, Economics and Politics, but it can be chosen along with any subject.

History at HE level

Pure History remains a very popular choice at university level. Employers appreciate the skills that historians develop and it is still seen as an academically rigorous discipline. You will often find that History forms a part of other degree subjects too. Related courses include Economic History, International History, Political History, Ancient History and many others. In general, you would probably need A level History to get on to these courses, but not in every case.

A degree in History?

Like most degrees these days, History can be quite varied and flexible in its content. However, most degrees will have some core subjects (usually studied in the first year) and then have the option of allowing students to specialise in certain areas by choosing particular modules. The options usually include most areas of British, European and World History and students will often consider issues such as theories of history as well as actual historical periods.

Combining History with other degree subjects

History is also combined with many other disciplines to form a joint degree. Such courses include Geography and History, Politics and History, German and History and so on. The possibilities are endless because the vast majority of arts, humanities and social science subjects at degree level always include a lot of emphasis on historical context: in this way, History is an ideal accompaniment for any of them.

Foundation degrees and Diplomas

There is currently there is no separate History Foundation degree. Similarly, there are no BTEC Higher National qualifications available in History.

History and your future career

Non-graduate jobs

Many employers requiring A levels do not really mind which subjects applicants have. In that sense, History A level is a good a choice as any. In fact, there may be some non-graduate areas of work where this A level is still more useful than some others because of the particular skills gained and knowledge acquired. These include:

- Administrative work (such as areas of the civil service)
- Management
- Sales
- Marketing
- Working as an assistant in a museum or gallery.

Graduate jobs: directly related to History

History-related occupations include the following, but many require Further Education or training:

- **Academic librarian/information manager/records manager:** responsible for the acquisition, organisation and dissemination of information and materials within the library system or information unit.
- **Archaeologist:** studies human past through material remains.
- **Archivist:** acquires, selects, arranges, stores, preserves and retrieves records not in current use but deemed to be of historical value.
- **Genealogist:** traces and charts lines of descent or family trees. Possibility of freelance work.
- **Museum/art gallery curator:** responsible for the care and improvement of a collection including exhibitions, catalogues and acquisitions.
- **Secondary school teacher:** teaches history to 11–18 year olds in schools.

Graduate jobs where History could be useful

The following represent some of the other potential areas of employment:

- **Arts administrator:** brings together artists and audiences to support and generate artistic activity.
- **Civil Service Fast Streamer:** through fast stream entry graduates are involved in helping senior staff, and through them ministers, to formulate and implement policy. Graduates also enter as junior managers (formerly executive officers), with administrative and management responsibilities.
- **Journalist:** gathers and presents news and features to the public.

- **Marketing executive:** manages the marketing of a product or service from research and development through to the launch. This can include promotion and advertising to the public or businesses.
- **Primary school teacher:** develops and fosters the appropriate skills and social abilities to enable the optimum development of children, within the framework of the National Curriculum.
- **Sales executive:** promotes and maximises sales of a company's products or services in designated markets. Also identifies new markets and new business and acts as liaison between producer and the retailer or wholesaler.

Further information

The Council for British Archaeology   www.britarch.ac.uk

The Historical Association   www.history.org.uk

The Museums Association   www.museumsassociation.org

HISTORY OF ART

The History of Art is a fairly specialised subject introducing students to a wealth of art, architecture and decorative arts from the most some of the world's most famous artists. In practice, most of these of artists come from Western Europe especially those from the Italian Renaissance. As well learning about some of the techniques used by artists, students learn about the historical, social, religious and political context in which the pieces of art were produced. What themes are repeated in Art throughout the centuries? Which artists have been the most influential? How did the political hierarchy patronise artists to further their political ends?

Subject options

The only exam board that currently offers this A level is AQA, and the outline of the course is given below.

Main elements of the course

Unit 1: Visual analysis and interpretation

An introduction to the methodology and terminology of the history of art.

Unit 2: Themes in history of art

Students learn some significant art historical themes from classical Greece to the art of the 20th Century.

Unit 3: Investigation and interpretation (1)

Schools have the option of teaching any of the following:

- Art and Architecture in 15th Century Europe
- Art and Architecture in 17th Century Europe
- Art and Architecture in 19th Century Europe
- Art and Architecture in Europe and the United States of America 1946–2000.

Unit 4: Investigation and interpretation (2)

Schools have the option of teaching any of the following:

- Art and Architecture in 13th and 14th Century Europe
- Art and Architecture in 16th Century Europe
- Art and Architecture in 18th Century Europe
- Art and Architecture in Europe and the United States of America 1900–1945.

AS students complete units one and two; A2 candidates complete units one to four.

How is A/AS level History of Art taught and assessed?

As you could imagine, this subject involves lots of looking at images in books, on slides, on stained glass windows, in museums and galleries. There may be visits to places of art-historical interest. There is of course the usual classroom and textbook work as with most other subjects. Students are also encouraged to do independent reading to support their learning in the classroom. Assessment is written examination.

Choosing other subjects to go with History of Art

History of Art obviously goes well with History, Art and Design, English Literature, Classics. However, you can do this subject alongside almost any other so long as they satisfy the entry requirements for Higher Education, if that's what you decide to do.

History of Art at HE level

Most universities will not insist on A level History of Art, but they will prefer your subject choices to include English, History or a foreign language.

A degree in History of Art

A degree in this subject will really develop some of the themes explored at A level. Many courses include some fieldwork or visits to places relevant to the course. Examples of core and optional modules taken from a degree course are as follows:

Core modules

- Introduction to the history of art
- The classical tradition
- Theory and historiography.

Optional modules

- Impacts of the late antique c. 350–850
- The art of Anglo-Saxon England, c. 600–1066
- The age of the cathedrals: architecture in England c. 1050–1250
- East and West: art of the Crusading era
- European art of the High Middle Ages
- Art and patronage in 15th Century Florence
- Art in Venice: from Bellini to Tintoretto
- The art of Holy Russia: painting, piety and power in the principality of Moscow c. 1500–1680.

Combining Art History with other degree subjects

Art History is most commonly combined with English and History and sometimes they are the only combinations that institutions offer. Sometimes though, one sees the subject being combined with Classics, Archaeology or a foreign language.

Foundation degrees and Diplomas

There are no Foundation degrees in this subject but there are some in the humanities-related field as well as in languages, literature and culture which may include some references to the History of Art. There are currently no BTEC Higher Nationals in this subject.

History of Art and your future career

Non-graduate jobs

It may be possible to get a starter position in an auction house, gallery, museum, design company or the antiques business straight after A levels, but increasingly some of these professions are being seen as graduate entry. Other areas are open to you too and you don't have to think of history of art-related jobs only.

Graduate jobs directly related to History of Art

Most jobs directly related to the history of art require some form of further study, training or experience. Some of the jobs you could consider are listed below.

- **Auctioneer/valuer, fine arts:** identifies and values pieces of art, secures them for auctions and compiles catalogues. Also organises, attends and supervises auctions.
- **Historic buildings inspector/conservation officer:** inspects and reports on buildings of special architectural or historic interest to ensure their preservation and conservation.
- **Museum/art gallery curator:** responsible for the development and management of a collection, including acquisitions, cataloguing and storage, as well as marketing and presentation to the public through exhibitions, documentation and talks.
- **Museum education officer:** creates a link between a museum and audiences and develops learning opportunities and materials for children or adults in or outside formal education.
- **Museum/gallery exhibitions officer:** researches, organises, selects objects for and mounts exhibitions in museums or art galleries.
- **Museum/gallery conservator/restorer:** assesses and analyses the condition of a particular type of object or art. Carries out treatments to arrest decay while maintaining the object's integrity.

Graduate jobs where History of Art could be useful

- **Archivist:** manages a public or private collection of records (or images) which have historic value by selecting, acquiring, cataloguing and preserving them.
- **Arts administrator:** supports, generates and is responsible for the organisation of artistic activities and organisations. Duties include budgeting and marketing.

- **Event organiser:** researches, organises and publicises events which allow businesses and customers to meet. Responsible for choosing venues, liaising with exhibitors, contractors, caterers and press.
- **Heritage manager:** responsible for the conservation and all aspects of public access to heritage sites. Develops and markets a site to visitors, while preserving its character.
- **Heritage officer/interpreter:** communicates the significance of a place or object to visitors through exhibitions, displays, re-enactments and publications.
- **Tourism officer:** develops and promotes tourist attractions to visitors and the tourism industry through events, marketing campaigns and information.

Further information

The Association of Art Historians   www.aah.org.uk

The Institute of Conservation   www.icon.org.uk

H. Honour and J. Fleming, *A World History of Art*
(Laurence King Publishers, 2005)

HOME ECONOMICS

In days gone by, if you studied Home Economics, you learned all about how to cook and how to work with textiles. Today, Home Economics as a post-16 subject is focused on food, nutrition and health and how these relate to the society in which we live. What are the nutritional properties of proteins and fat? How does diet affect life expectancy and quality of life? How dangerous are bacteria, additives and agricultural chemicals? As a student of Home Economics, these are just some of the questions you may debate and answer during the course.

Subject options

This subject is available at GCE A/AS level, and is offered by AQA, OCR and CCEA. Note that each Home Economics course can have a slightly different focus.

A/AS level

The following is based on the CCEA specification.

Unit 1: Nutrition for optimal health

Macro and micro-nutrients and other dietary constituents; nutritional requirements and dietary recommendations.

Unit 2: Priority health issues

Current research in relation to diet and health; mental health; sexual health; targets, strategies, initiatives and campaigns for optimising health are also studied.

Unit 3: Consumer issues

Food safety issues; ethical issues for consumers; financial management issues for consumers; consumer information; consumer protection and redress.

Unit 4: Research-based assignment

Students research an area covered in the specification above and produce a 4,000-word report about it.

Assessment is by a mixture of final examinations (written papers) and possibly a coursework element. AS candidates complete units one and two; if you are taking the A2 course, then you complete all of the units.

Choosing other subjects to go with Home Economics

This subject goes well with many others including Sociology, Health and Social Care and PE/Sport.

Home Economics at HE level

There are a few Home Economics courses at HE level. You don't necessarily need to have studied Home Economics at A/AS level to get a place. If you're interested in related subjects such as Nutrition and Dietetics, then most universities prefer you to have studied science subjects beforehand.

A degree in Home Economics?

Some university courses are called Home Economics and others are called Food Design and Technology. Courses generally have a core component and some options. Examples include:

- Consumer law
- Food, nutrition and health
- Food tourism and gastronomy
- Food science
- Media and food
- Principles of human nutrition.

Combining Home Economics with other degree subjects

Potentially, and depending on your pre-university subjects, Home Economics could go well with Law, Nutrition and Dietetics, Business, Sport/PE and Leisure Studies.

Foundation degrees and Diplomas

There are no Foundation degrees specifically in Home Economics, but there are some subjects that have some related content, such as Hospitality, Tourism and Leisure Services as well as Sports Studies/Science. There are also BTEC Higher Nationals in Hospitality Management and in Health and Social Care.

Home Economics and your future career

Non-graduate jobs

There are a few jobs that students could go into that are related to Home Economics straight after a Level 3 qualification. These include working in hospitality and catering, perhaps for a chain of hotels; if you're interested in the consumer side of the subject then it would be possible to start off in a junior administrative role in a consumer agency (such as the Food Standards Agency).

Graduate jobs directly related to Home Economics

There are very few careers where a first degree in Home Economics is essential, or directly relevant. There are some jobs which are closely related to a Home Economics degree but they may also require particular A level subjects, experience or further training. The following are most closely related to Home Economics:

- **Dietitian:** this work will appeal if you're attracted to the nutritional aspects of food science. It involves both a therapeutic and preventative role. Qualification as a dietitian is a two-year postgraduate Diploma course. Candidates need to have a good knowledge of biochemistry and physiology, as well as an ability to relate well to people.
- **Food technologist or scientist, product/process development:** works in three main areas: product development, quality assurance and retailing – with a potential overlap between all three. Aims to produce food which is safe and nutritious with a consistent flavour, colour and texture. Develops new, and modifies existing products and processes. Works in industry, but also government and local authority food inspection departments.

Graduate jobs where a degree in Home Economics could be useful

- **Industrial buyer or retail buyer:** procures or purchases the highest quality and appropriate quantity of goods and services at the most competitive rate to meet user need according to specified criteria. The work requires continuous development of market knowledge and contacts for new products and services.
- **Production manager:** takes responsibility for all stages of the manufacture of a product including the planning, coordination and control of industrial processes. This can present a range of challenges, both technically and in terms of managing production workers.
- **Quality assurance manager (QA):** acts to ensure that each product is of the correct materials, correctly made, properly packed, transported, labelled and up to standard when released to the customer. Responsible for maintaining the quality system and giving advice on any required changes and their implementation. The QA also provides training, tools and techniques to enable others to achieve quality.

Further information

Institute of Consumer Science   www.icsc.org.uk

INFORMATION, COMMUNICATION AND TECHNOLOGY (ICT)

Depending on the specific type of course you take, ICT introduces you to a whole range of practical and academic issues relating to computing and information systems. The subject equips you with some excellent skills whether or not you want to work in the ICT field while still preparing you for HE should you choose to go down that route. What is an information system? How are ICT projects managed effectively? How do I create a website? How do I design a spreadsheet? These are just some of the questions that will be answered by studying ICT.

Subject options

This subject is available as GCE A/AS level and as Applied GCE A/AS level. You may also be interested in BTEC Nationals in IT and Computing, as well as A/AS level Computing (see the entry on Computing for detailed information). From September 2008, there will also be a new Diploma in IT available.

A/AS level

The overall aim of this course is to encourage students to develop an understanding of the fundamentals of ICT and to provide the knowledge and skills suitable for participation in an evolving information-based society. The course provides a focus to develop these skills whilst ensuring that students acquire a sound knowledge of ICT. As a student of A level ICT, you are given the opportunity to develop interpersonal, academic and technical skills which will help you to meet career challenges in the future. What is the most appropriate use of software for different purposes? These are just some of the questions that students of this subject are asked to consider.

For an exact definition of the AS and A2 syllabus you will be studying, you should consult your school, college or the exam board itself. All the exam boards cover the same topics but some of them are grouped together slightly differently. The main elements of most ICT courses are:

Information, systems and communications
The building blocks of information systems.

Structured practical ICT tasks
Students learn practical skills in design, software development, testing and implementation.

Practical applications of ICT using standard/generic applications software
Students learn about standard applications software as well as online relational and non-relational databases.

Communications technology and its application
This aspect focuses on how IT technology is used as a communication tool between individuals and businesses. Issues such as networking and further uses of ICT are explored.

ICT project

Students work on their own project throughout the course. This is usually an IT solution to a problem encountered by a user.

ICT systems and systems management

This element of the course focuses in more detail on IT and Communication systems for business as well as ICT solutions to many business problems.

AS students study two core modules and carry out a project. A2 students complete five modules and a project.

Applied A/AS level

The Applied A/AS level in ICT has many of the same elements that the traditional GCE course has with a number of main differences. First, the applied course goes into more detail about some of the ICT functions/areas studied and how they can be applied in 'real life'; second, students can take options with a more specialised vocational focus with a larger choice of options to choose from; and third, the assessment for the applied subject is much more based on producing portfolios of evidence rather than written exams. As can be seen from the selection of modules below, the applied course is much more about 'how to do' things rather than theoretical or historical considerations:

- Advanced spreadsheet design
- Creating a website
- Data handling
- ICT solutions
- Publishing
- Programming
- Web management.

Advanced Diploma

An overview of content of the Diploma in Information and communication Technology is given below.

In line with the demands of the modern IT profession, the Diploma in Information Technology focuses on three main themes: Business, People and Technology.

1. Business: how organisations work and the role technology can play.

2. People: how to work well with other people.

3. Technology: how to create technology solutions.

Assessment

Work experience. With a Diploma you'll get to learn all about your chosen subject through a range of core and optional subjects. You'll also get at least 10 days' work experience. This is a great way to use the skills you have learn in the classroom and experience what work is like from the inside.

Student Project. You will also be required to complete a Student Project. This is to demonstrate the skills and knowledge that you have learnt on your Diploma course. You can choose your own project to show off your skills in the best light. It will help you bring your subject to life and express your creativity in a work context.

Personal, learning and thinking skills. All Diploma students are encouraged to develop skills like teamwork and self management as part of the course. You will learn how to express yourself confidently and apply your knowledge and skills creatively in a work environment.

The Diploma in Information Technology does not mean you have to pursue a career in this sector. A Diploma gives you the relevant, transferable skills that will be welcomed by colleges, universities and employers.

How is ICT taught and assessed?

A/AS level

You don't need to have any prior knowledge of IT to study this subject but a practical mind, an interest in the subject and good spatial awareness will help you in the subject. Teaching is done by a mixture of classroom input and practical work in the IT lab. Assessment is through written exams and a practical coursework project.

Applied A/AS level

Teaching is similar to the traditional A level but there is a much more practice-based emphasis. Real-life case studies, visits to organisations using IT in interesting ways and talks from IT professionals are often part of the teaching methods used. Assessment is mainly by internally assessed portfolios of evidence with the occasional written exam. There are four possible routes for gaining an award in this subject: AS single award (three units); AS double award (six units); A level single award (six units); A level double award (12 units).

Choosing other subjects to go with ICT

Good supporting subjects for this one would include Business, Maths, Geography, Accounting, Computing and IT and Design and Technology. However, you should make sure your focus isn't too narrow as this could affect your ability to get a place on an HE course.

ICT at HE level

Students don't necessarily need to have already studied ICT to take it at a higher level but some universities may specify at least one scientific or technical A level. There are some courses based solely on information systems but they tend to be at postgraduate level. Some courses are very theoretical; others are very practical or applied in their emphasis. You should always check the specific nature of a course before applying.

A degree in ICT?

Most degree courses aren't called ICT but Computer Science or a variation thereof. Computing courses, even if they are theoretical, will consider how IT is applied to business, industry and research. There are usually core components in the first year with some flexibility in the final two years depending on your interests. The kinds of issues considered include:

- Bioinformatics
- Communications and networks
- Computational finance
- Information security
- Logic programming
- Managing information systems
- Object-oriented software engineering
- Object-oriented modelling
- Web and internet technologies.

Assessment is via a combination of final exams, coursework and project work.

Combining ICT degree with other subjects

The different combinations possible with the subject are numerous, but some joint programmes offered by some IT/Computer Science Departments at university include:

- Computer Science with Artificial Intelligence
- Computer Science with French
- Computer Science with management
- Computer Science and Maths
- Computer Science and Physics.

Foundation degrees and Diplomas

There are many Foundation degrees in IT-related subjects, examples being Business Information Technology, Web Development, Design for Digital Technologies and many more. Find a course at www.ucas.com. There are also BTEC Higher Nationals available in Computing.

ICT and your future career

Non-graduate jobs

Given that nearly every organisation needs computers now, you will be an asset if you have an advanced understanding of them. So in that sense, there are quite a few junior positions that you could apply for. You may even be able to get work in IT support in some organisations without any further qualifications.

Graduate jobs directly related ICT

Some of the more common job titles used include the following.

- **Applications developer:** writes and modifies programs to enable a computer to carry out specific tasks, such as stock control or payroll, typically for technical, commercial and business users.
- **Database administrator:** responsible for the usage, accuracy, efficiency, security, maintenance and development of an organisation's computerised databases.
- **Information technology consultant:** gives independent and objective advice on how best to use information technology to solve business problems.
- **Software engineer:** specifies, develops, documents and maintains computer software programs in order to meet client or employer need. Usually works as part of a team.
- **Systems developer:** sets up the computer operating systems and standard software services essential to the operation of any computer.
- **Systems designer:** takes the specification for the requirements of a computer system and designs the system including hardware, software, communications, installation, testing and maintenance.
- **Web designer:** responsible for the design, layout and coding of web pages. This is known as the 'front-end' of websites, as it is what the user sees. The work may also involve multimedia activities such as video clips, music and other media. Web designers are also known as web producers, internet engineers and multimedia architects.

Graduate jobs where ICT would be useful

Information technology is being used in every single sector of the economy. The following jobs will make some use of your IT background.

- **IT sales professional:** gives technical advice and guidance to customers pre- or post-installation of their computer systems; normally works in conjunction with sales representatives for a computer manufacturer.
- **Magazine journalist:** researches and writes news and feature articles which are suited to the magazine's reader profile.
- **Recruitment consultant:** particularly for the IT sector. Obtains the brief for job vacancies from clients, then matches candidates with the relevant qualities to these vacancies and arranges interviews with the clients.
- **Secondary school teacher:** teaches one, or more, specialist subject/s to classes of secondary pupils aged 11–18. IT is currently a shortage subject.

Further information

The British Computer Society	www.bcs.org
The Computer Information Centre	www.compinfo-center.com
Game On – advice on working in the Computer Games industry	www.blitzgames.com/gameon/

LAW

This subject gives you a good insight into how the English legal system operates. It examines how laws come into being and how they are upheld. As well as the systems of law and justice, students are introduced to the many different types of Law that are practised in the UK as well as their implications for everyday life. In the study of law, students may also engage with some important and interesting issues such as human rights, euthanasia, the impact of EU legislation on our lives and much more.

Subject options

This subject is available at GCE A/AS level, but there are also elements of law in the BTEC Nationals in Business.

AS/A2 level

For an exact definition of the AS and A2 syllabus you will be studying, you should consult your school, college or the exam board itself. This subject is offered by AQA, WJEC and OCR. The specifications cover more or less the same ground – differences are mainly in how the material is organised and what the modules are called. The following outline is based on the new AQA syllabus.

Unit 1: Law-making and the legal system
Parliamentary law making; delegated legislation; statutory interpretation; judicial precedent; the civil courts and other forms of dispute resolution; the criminal courts and lay people; the legal profession and other sources of advice and funding; the judiciary.

Unit 2: The concept of liability
Underlying principles of criminal liability; the courts: procedure and sentencing; liability in negligence; the courts: procedure and damages; formation of contract; breach of contract.

Unit 3: Criminal law or contract law
Murder; voluntary manslaughter; involuntary manslaughter; non-fatal offences against the person; defences; formation of contracts; contract terms; discharge of contract.

Unit 4: Criminal law or tort and concepts of law
Criminal law (offences against property): theft and robbery; burglary; blackmail; fraud; making off without payment; criminal damage; defences.

Law of tort: negligence; occupier's liability; nuisance and escape of dangerous things; vicarious liability; defences; remedies.

Concepts of law: law and morals; law and justice; judicial creativity; fault; balancing conflicting interests.

How is A/AS level Law taught and assessed?

Students don't have to have studied GCSE Law to do well at this subject because A/AS level Law is essentially learning a lot of facts about the legal system and then analysing what is learned. There is a lot of reading and writing for this subject – as there is when working as a lawyer! – but don't let that put you off because for some it is a fascinating subject. All the work is assessed by exams at various points in the course and there is no coursework for this subject.

Choosing other subjects to go with Law

Law goes well with many other subjects including arts and humanities subjects such as English and History. It also goes well with other finance-related subjects such as Accounting, Business and Economics. Many students also study Law alongside a modern foreign language.

Law at HE level

Most universities do not ask that you've studied A level Law to study it at HE level, but they will look for sound traditional subjects. In some respects, if you want to study Law at university, you may be safer choosing traditional academic subjects rather than more business focused ones, even though the practice of law is largely a commercial affair. In fact, some leading universities have included A/AS level Law on the list of subjects that they don't consider academically rigorous enough. Always check beforehand if you intend going on to Higher Education.

A degree in Law

A Law degree is usually called LLB Laws (Bachelor of Laws) and it will cover the basics in the first year, expanding what is taught at A/AS level. In the second and third years, students have the chance to take some more specialised units aligned to their personal or career interests. Core courses at university level usually include:

- Criminal law
- Elements of contract law
- European law
- Public law.

Special options could cover a whole range of law-related topics, but the following is a small sample:

- Banking law
- Copyright and designs
- Human Rights law
- International trade law
- Medical law
- Russian legal institutions.

Combining Law with other degree subjects

This really varies from university to university, but some common combinations include:

- Law and Accounting
- Law and Business
- Law and a Modern Foreign Language
- Law and Sociology
- Law and Philosophy.

Foundation degrees and Diplomas

There are many legally-related Foundation courses available which you can find at www.ucas.com. Edexcel currently offers a BTEC Higher National in Business Law.

Law and your future career

Non-graduate jobs

Law is seen by employers as an academically sound and rigorous subject and therefore students with this subject under their belt will be in demand. However it's also important to emphasise other transferable skills such as problem-solving, analytical skills and writing skills. Jobs working in law are mainly reserved for graduates but you may be able to work in junior positions in legal contexts such as administration in a law firm.

Graduate jobs directly related to Law

Solicitor/Barrister: requires postgraduate qualifications and training.

Graduate Jobs where a degree in Law could be useful

There are a number of careers where legal knowledge and skills can be put to use.

- **Advice worker:** employed by local and central government and the voluntary sector. Advice and information is provided to the public or to special client groups, in person, in writing and over the telephone.
- **Ancillary legal professions:** If you are attracted to work in the legal field you could consider an ancillary role. A law degree is not required and postgraduate qualifications are not necessary for all of them. Occupations include barrister's clerk, legal executive (England and Wales), licensed conveyancer and legal secretary.
- **Chartered accountant:** works to ensure effective use of financial resources of individuals or organisations. Can include auditing, financial management and planning and giving financial advice.
- **Civil Service fast streamer:** employed in all government departments. Some have legal responsibilities, e.g. Lord Chancellor's Office, CPS.
- **Excise and inland customs officer:** involves regulating the entry of certain goods through ports and airports; controlling the movement of dutiable materials within the UK and the assessment and collection of VAT.

- **Immigration officer, passport control:** meets passengers and assesses their eligibility for admission.
- **Inspector of health and safety:** inspects factories, quarries, offices, farms and other places of work. Ensures working conditions and machinery are safe and comply with regulations.
- **Local government administrator:** employed in all departments in local authorities.
- **Police officer:** maintains law and order; protects persons and property; prevents crime; deals with emergencies.
- **Prison officer:** keeps people committed by the courts in custody; looks after them with humanity and helps them lead law-abiding and useful lives in custody and after release.
- **Probation officer:** supervises people placed under probation orders and other forms of suspension and those released from custody.
- **Tax inspector:** determines the tax liabilities of individuals and businesses on behalf of the Inland Revenue, including assessment and examination of accounts.
- **Trading standards officer:** promotes, maintains and develops fair trading through inspecting premises, advising traders and consumers and investigating complaints.

Further information

The Bar Council   www.barcouncil.org.uk

The Law Careers Advice Network   www.lcan.org.uk

Law Society   www.lawsociety.org.uk

LEISURE STUDIES (APPLIED)

This is an 'applied' A/AS level and has a number of main aims: to give students an insight into the leisure industry within the UK and EU; to equip students with some of the skills and techniques to enable them to develop a career in the leisure industry; and to encourage an understanding of the benefits of a healthy and active lifestyle. It is ideal for those students who want a broad background in the Leisure and Recreation industry, and the course will allow them to progress to Further and Higher Education or employment. This sector is a fast growing one. People have more disposable income to spend on leisure and recreation than ever before (the number of health clubs is at a record high) and the industry needs well-qualified people.

Subject options

This subject is available at applied A/AS level offered by AQA, OCR and Edexcel. They cover very similar ground, the main differences are the title of modules and the way the material is organised and structured. There will also be a new Advanced Diploma in Sport and Leisure available from 2010.

The following outline is based on the AQA specification.

- Unit 1: The leisure industry today
- Unit 2: A people business
- Unit 3: Getting it right in the leisure industry
- Unit 4: Leisure facilities
- Unit 5: Lifestyles and life stages
- Unit 6: Leisure organisations
- Unit 7: Fitness training for sport
- Unit 8: Leisure in action
- Unit 9: Working in the people business
- Unit 10: Current issues
- Unit 11: Leisure and the media
- Unit 12: Lifestyle management
- Unit 13: Leisure in the community
- Unit 14: Outdoor leisure.

How is A/AS level Leisure Studies taught and assessed?

You need no prior knowledge of this subject to take this course, however having studied GCSE Leisure and Tourism may be an advantage. As well as classroom work, students may visit different types of leisure and recreation organisations, and do lots of independent research about the sector. Assessment is by a combination of externally set and marked written exams and internally assessed portfolios of evidence. For instance your assessment task for a unit may be to write a report, carry out an investigation or sit a written exam. There are four possible routes for gaining an award in this subject: AS single award (three units); AS double award (six units); A level single award (six units); A level double award (12 units)

Choosing other subjects to go with Leisure Studies

This subject goes well with other 'applied' subjects such as Business Studies, ICT and Travel and Tourism. *NB: if you choose to combine Leisure Studies with Travel and Tourism there may be too much overlap and exam boards may not permit the combination, so check with your school.*

Leisure Studies at HE level

There are different types of leisure and recreation related degrees such as Leisure and Recreation Management, Sports Science and Recreation and Leisure Studies. Check the entry requirements for each course as there may be quite a bit of variation between them. Many courses are sandwich courses, meaning that students work for a year in the leisure and recreation industry and some point during their course. Some courses offer a year abroad option.

A degree in Leisure Studies?

The most common type of degree in this area is Leisure (and Recreation) Management. Sometimes it comes under the Business School part of a university and sometimes not. Some of the features of such a course would usually include:

- Foundations of leisure
- Leisure analysis and information technology
- Leisure business
- Leisure facility management
- Leisure policy
- Sport Industry
- Sport Tourism.

Combining Leisure Studies with other degree subjects

This depends on individual departments, but possible joint subjects include Business/ Management, Accounting, Nutrition, Sports Science, Computing and possibly a few others.

Foundation degrees and Diplomas

There are many Foundation degree courses in the field of Hospitality, Tourism and Leisure Services. You can search for these at www.ucas.com.

Leisure Studies and your future career

Non-graduate jobs

There is a great demand for staff in this ever-changing sector and therefore it's possible for students with an A level in this subject to start working at junior supervisory levels in a variety of settings. As well as knowledge gained from the course, students need to emphasise their skills in teamwork, problem-solving and using initiative. As their careers develop students may want to consider vertical progression through a relevant on-the-job qualification.

Graduate jobs directly related to a degree in Leisure studies

- **Betting shop manager:** responsible for running a betting shop profitably, organising, recruiting and training staff, security and for ensuring fast and accurate payment of winnings.
- **Fitness centre manager:** responsible for day-to-day running of the business, design of activity programme, budgeting, customer care, market research and marketing, membership sales and staff supervision, development and training.
- **Leisure centre manager:** promotes, organises and runs a leisure centre in either the public or private sector. Effectively in charge of several small business operations: catering, personnel, customer relations, bars, promotions and financial planning.
- **Lifestyle consultant:** carries out fitness assessments, provides physical fitness and lifestyle health programmes in mainly private sector health clubs or hotels, but sometimes in organisations wishing to provide facilities for their employees.
- **Outdoor pursuits manager:** responsible for provision of facilities and instruction in a range of outdoor activities. Duties include: staff management; health and safety of clients; planning day and evening activities; handling customer complaints.
- **Sports administrator:** works within a sport's governing body or the Sports Council, dealing with financial, organisational and administrative aspects of their sport. May involve national travel to support events.
- **Sports development officer:** encourages people to take part in sport by promoting their sport to target groups. Usually works for a governing body or professional association.
- **Theme park manager:** involves recruiting staff, dealing with finances, ensuring high standards of presentation and service, marketing the park and liaising with other management staff.
- **Tourism officer:** plans and co-ordinates leisure activities, usually on a geographic basis for a local authority.

Graduate jobs where a degree in Leisure Studies could be useful

- **Event organiser:** organises conferences/events/exhibitions, liaises with clients, is responsible for administration and manages staff and contractors.
- **Further Education lecturer or Higher Education lecturer:** teaching through lectures, tutorials and practical skills classes on aspect(s) of leisure and recreation.
- **Newspaper journalist:** responsible for news or information gathering and reporting. Involves developing contacts, interviewing personalities, attending press conferences and producing copy to a deadline.
- **Public relations officer:** promotes events, sponsorship deals and presents sport and leisure topics to the media.
- **Retail manager:** specialist sports retail companies could offer management posts in buying, merchandising or store management.

Further information

Fitness Industry Association (FIA)   www.fia.org.uk

Institute of Leisure and Amenities
Management (ILAM)   www.ilam.co.uk

Institute of Sport and Recreation
Management (ISRM)   www.isrm.co.uk

MATHEMATICS

Mathematics is at the core of many of the things we know about life, about the world around us, even the movements of substances inside our bodies. What's the best way of predicting the likelihood of something happening? How fast is a particular planet spinning? How does the economy work in detail? How much profit will a company make? Trying to answer any of these questions will to a certain extent involve the use of numbers and mathematics. This subject builds on the basics learned at GCSE as well as introducing new concepts and new ways for solving particular problems.

Subject options

This subject is available at GCE A/AS level and at Advanced Extension Award level. GCE A/AS level statistics is also offered by OCR.

A/AS level

Mathematics is really divided between 'pure maths' and 'applied maths' (applying the subject to different contexts and uses. The exam boards tend to give schools and colleges some choice about the options students choose in the different mathematical areas. For an exact definition of the AS and A2 syllabus you will be studying, you should consult your school, college or the exam board itself.

The main topics are as follows:

Pure mathematics
This is the foundation for what you do in other areas and includes topics such as trigonometry; quadratic equations; vectors; differential equations; complex numbers; matrices.

Mechanics
This aspect focuses on the way objects move and looks at physical forces. Topics studied include Newton's law of motion; linear momentum; centre of mass; equilibrium; energy; work and power; elasticity and inertia.

Statistics and probability
Collecting and presenting data; working out valid sample sizes from a group of data; probability; variables; mean value and spread; hypothesis testing.

Discrete mathematics
Discrete maths is used in computer science, management and economics and includes things such as algorithms; networks; linear programming; game theory and dynamic programming.

Those studying for the AS awards generally take three units and those going for the Advanced award take six units.

Advanced Extension Award

The AEA in Mathematics, aimed at the top 10 per cent of students, will assess the ability to solve a range of unfamiliar problems, problems that can be solved from students' knowledge gained at A level. Students answer a series of questions in examination conditions and will be assessed on the extent to which they can apply and communicate their understanding of mathematics (e.g. problem-solving and deductive reasoning; critical analysis; evaluation and synthesis).

For detailed information and examples of past papers, see Edexcel's website.

How is A/AS level Maths taught and assessed?

To do well in this subject, students realistically need to have achieved a Grade A or B at GCSE level. This is partly because a sound grasp of previously learned concepts is needed in order to make real progress at A level. There is a lot of class work, with students learning new theories and then doing practice examples. There is also lots of using graphs and charts, equations and calculator work. Coursework is an option for this course, otherwise it is all assessed through written examinations.

Choosing other subjects to go with Mathematics

Maths goes well with subjects such as Physics, Chemistry, Business, IT/Computing, Chemistry and Biology. However, it is often combined with other subjects such as a modern foreign language or Music.

Mathematics at HE level

To study Mathematics at a higher level, you will need to have achieved a good grade at A level in the subject. Degree courses can focus on different areas of the Mathematics such as Pure Mathematics or Applied Mathematics.

A degree in Mathematics?

Most degree courses have core modules and optional elements. A sample is given below.

Sample core courses:

- Calculus
- Geometry
- Introduction to dynamical systems
- Linear methods.

Sample optional courses:

- Financial mathematics
- Quantum mechanics

- Space – time physics
- Thermodynamics and information theory.

Combining Mathematics with other degree subjects

Common joint degrees offered by universities include: French and Maths; Maths and Philosophy; Maths and Physics; Maths and Management; and Maths with Computer Science.

Foundation degrees and Diplomas

There are no Foundation degrees or BTEC Higher Nationals in Maths, but there are some in related areas such as Engineering and IT.

Mathematics and your future career

Non-graduate jobs

Mathematics is a very attractive subject to employers as there aren't many organisations that don't have to do some kind of mathematical work. It could be possible to get junior positions in retail, banking, insurance and many other areas straight after A levels.

Graduate jobs directly related to Maths

- **Actuarial work:** an actuary studies past events to predict future outcomes. This often involves the application of probability and statistics to financial affairs, especially life assurance, pensions and social security.
- **Economic and statistical work:** a statistician collects, analyses and interprets quantitative information. This work is carried out in many organisations and research establishments, notably the Civil Service, the Health Service and large industrial and commercial organisations.
- **Scientific research and development:** most openings are for applied mathematicians with relevant higher degrees, including information technology. Much of the work is carried out in multidisciplinary teams with other scientists.
- **Secondary school teacher:** you will normally have to undertake a PGCE before entering this field.

Graduate jobs where a degree in Mathematics could be useful

- **Accountancy:** employers of trainee accountants rarely specify degree disciplines, but all look for numeracy and literacy skills and the capacity to establish interpersonal relationships rapidly.
- **Insurance and pensions:** insurance companies offer many openings in addition to actuarial work, including investment analysis, systems technology and underwriting.

- **IT, economics, statistics and management services:** the employers of computer personnel are numerous, with the three main openings being found with users of the equipment, e.g. banks, oil companies and retail chains.
- **Management consultancy:** covers a wide range of applications and the type of work depends on the sector in which a graduate works. Competition for posts is fierce.
- **Retail banking and personal financial services:** The growth in applications of information technology has led to an increase in careers for graduates in areas covering communications, data processing and funds transfer.

Further information

The Institute of Mathematics
and its Applications   www.ima.org.uk

Maths Careers   www.mathscareers.org.uk

Royal Statistical Society (RSS)   www.rss.org.uk

MEDIA STUDIES

If you study Media, you can gain experience of both the theoretical and practical aspects of the subject. Whatever course you choose, there is usually a practical 'production' element, but some courses are more vocationally oriented than others. In the vocationally-oriented courses, students will study the working methods of current practitioners working in the media and gain an understanding of the different roles within the different areas of the media. In the more theoretical or 'academic' courses, students might focus more on the different genres of media such as film, documentary, the press and so on and carry out a critical analysis of them.

Subject options

Media Studies is available as a GCE A/AS level and Media: Communication and Production as an applied A/AS level. You might also consider BTEC Nationals in Media, Music and Performing Arts. *NB: Look at the entry on Film Studies for information on that and Moving Image Arts A level.*

Some students might be interested, too, in the new Advanced Diploma in Creative and Media, available from September 2008.

A/AS level

This subject is offered by OCR and AQA and the following outline is based on the latter's specification.

Unit 1: Investigating media
Media texts, concepts and contexts; e-media, broadcasting and print; printedcommunications; broadcast fiction; film fiction; documentary; lifestyle; music, news and sport.

Unit 2: Creating media
Preparing a practical production; technical and creative skills; knowledge of relevant conventions; target audiences; production media; evaluation.

Unit 3: Media: critical perspectives
Representations in the media; impact of digital media; cross media issues and debates; media theories.

Unit 4: Media: research and production
Research into a media text or theme; critical investigation; a linked production piece.

AS students complete units one and two; A2 students complete all four. Assessment is by a combination of written papers and media productions.

Applied A/AS level in Media: Communication and Production

The following is based on the Edexcel syllabus.

Unit no.	Unit Title
1	**Industries, texts and audience:** Students learn different ways of looking at and analysing the media – using ideas like narrative, representation and ideology.
2	**Skills development in media:** Developing the practical skills needed to create your own video and your own printed publicity for a video.
3	**Media production brief:** Using the skills and knowledge learned in Units 1 and 2 to prepare and create your own moving image product.
4	**Researching for media production:** Students develop an idea for a video product, and do some research into how viable the idea is from a professional and commercial point of view.
5	**Media production project:** Students make a film or video, and are expected to show very detailed evidence of how the production process was planned, using industry standard documentation techniques.
6	**Professional practice in the media industries:** Developing the knowledge of how media production works in different media industries as well as the moral, legal and ethical context of the industry.

No prior knowledge is needed for this course but candidates must have a good standard of literacy, some creative flair and an interest in the sector of work. Teaching is by a combination of classroom work, talks by people in the media field, possible work experience opportunities and practical work. Students may also spend a lot of time working with different media (e.g. print, TV, film, photography and so on). Assessment is via a combination of external examination and portfolios of evidence.

BTEC Nationals

BTEC Nationals in Media, Music and Performing Arts are available in three levels (Award, Certificate and Diploma), and are offered by Edexcel exam board.

The media-related topics available at the three levels are:

- Media Production*
- Media Production (Games Development)
- Media Production (Interactive Media)
- Media Production (Print-based Media)
- Media Production (Radio)

- Media Production (Sound Recording)
- Media Production (Television and Film).

* Media Production is not available at Award level

Assessment for this course is by completion of a portfolio of evidence, but students must spend a certain period of working in a relevant setting.

Advanced Diploma

The new Diploma in Creative and Media introduces different ways of learning and a broader range of subjects within one qualification than have been taught before. The close links with the business world prepare students for life after education.

You will learn important skills for the job market such as managing your time and working as a team. You will develop the ability to analyse, create and communicate. This will be through study of the creative industries as businesses, covering film to fashion, advertising to animation.

There are three levels of Diploma:

Usually starting in Year 10 or 12

- Foundation Diploma (equivalent to studying four or five GCSEs)
- Higher Diploma (equivalent to studying five or six GCSEs).

Usually starting in Year 12 or above

- Advanced Diploma (equivalent to studying three A levels).

A Progression Diploma will also be available, equivalent to two A levels, for those students who do not want to study for the full Advanced Diploma.

Choosing other subjects to go with Media Studies

This subject could go with almost any other GCE Advanced subject but if you want to study this subject at a higher level, then remember to check institutions' entry criteria so you know which subjects to use. Subjects that might go well include Communication and Culture and English.

Media/Media Studies at HE level

It's possible to study Media at a higher level in a variety of contexts including BTEC Higher Nationals, Foundation degrees and Bachelor degrees at universities. The important thing to remember is that some are very academic or theoretical whereas others are more vocationally specific.

A degree in Media Studies?

At university level, degrees in Media Studies can come in many different forms. On the one hand, they can focus on a very specific area of media (e.g. digital media, media production, print media, television media, interactive media and so on); on the other hand they can be general media related degrees such as Media Studies or Media Arts. An example of some options in a university Media Arts degree is given below:

- French cinema
- Hollywood star performances
- Media and history: holocaust
- Modernism
- Postmodern film and television
- Television genre
- Women's cinema.

Combining Media Studies with other degree subjects

Media is often combined with subjects such as English, a modern foreign language, IT and many others.

Foundation degrees and Diplomas

There are many different Foundation degrees available in specific areas of media.

Media Studies and your future career

Non-graduate jobs

A level Media will give you good skills and an insight into the profession. The media profession is notoriously difficult to get into though and you have to be prepared to make contacts and often work on an unpaid basis to build experience until you get your first break. Non-media careers are still open to you of course.

Graduate jobs directly related to Media Studies

Many students on these courses are interested in gaining employment in all aspects of the media industry. Careers in the media, however, are highly sought after and competition is likely to be fierce.

- **Broadcast assistant, radio:** assists with production and presentation of programmes for local and national radio stations.
- **Broadcasting presenter:** fronts the programme, specific responsibilities vary depending on the programme.
- **Journalism:** reports on news and other areas of interests for newspapers, periodicals, radio and TV.
- **Multimedia programmer:** researches, develops and produces materials for new media based company activities.
- **Programme researcher, broadcasting/film/video:** acts as an assistant producer with responsibility for conception and implementation of a programme.

- **Radio producer:** responsible for initiating ideas, selling these to commissioning editors and managing the technical and creative team to produce the final programme.
- **Television/film/video producer:** undertakes the artistic interpretation of materials and directs the production of shows/films.
- **Television production assistant:** provides organisational and secretarial services for programme director.

Graduate jobs where a degree in Media Studies could be useful

- **Advertising account executive:** takes overall responsibility for co-ordination, planning and organisation of advertising campaigns.
- **Arts administrator:** acts as facilitator for the exhibition and preservation of cultural forms including performing, visual and heritage arts.
- **Event organiser:** identifies potential business, researches, writes, plans and runs all types of conferences on behalf of a client or own organisation.
- **Information officer/manager:** ensures effective communication of information relating to a particular field of interest.
- **Market research executive:** undertakes systematic research to determine the potential market for a product or service.
- **Public relations account executive:** PR agencies work for their clients in presenting their image to the public. They decide on strategies to be used and which media would be the most effective.

Further information

The British Film Institute   www.bfi.org.uk/education

Skillset   www.skillset.org; www.skillsformedia.com

Useful website for media students   www.englishandmedia.com

T. O'Sullivan, B. Dutton and P. Raynes,
Studying the Media (Hodder Arnold, 2003)

MODERN LANGUAGES

There are many modern languages that can be studied at A level including French, German, Spanish, Italian, Portuguese, Urdu, Chinese, Dutch, Gujurati, Persian and quite a few more. The study of a foreign language at A level not only allows you to communicate with people from other countries, it also gives students an insight into the cultures and histories of the countries where the language is spoken. If you studied French, for instance, you could also end up studying Impressionist painting or other aspects of France's history or culture. If you enjoy communicating, learning new words and have a talent for remembering things, then studying a modern language could be for you.

Subject options

You can study a modern foreign language at GCE A/AS level. You can also study for an AEA.

A/AS level

Irrespective of the language you choose or the exam board your school or college uses, your course programme will include the following elements.

Speaking

You will be expected to converse regularly in the language, learn new vocabulary and verbs. You may also have role-plays to take part in. In the oral exams, you may have to make a presentation.

Listening

Students often find the listening part of learning a new language difficult. Throughout the course, you will listen to the language in different contexts such as news reports, song lyrics and conversations.

Reading

You will also have to do a lot of reading of different types of materials: this could be newspapers, literary texts, business letters, emails and so on.

Writing

The kind of writing skills you may need to develop as part of this A level include judging the right form and tone for a particular piece of written communication as well as ensuring it is grammatically and linguistically sound. Tasks such as writing a reply to a letter, making a job application, or writing a promotional leaflet may all be included.

Aspects of culture and society

Some foreign language courses also include a separate element on learning about the culture and society of the country where the language is predominantly spoken. This could be related to literature, the environment, the media, healthcare issues and many other topics.

Advanced Extension Award

This level is for students in the top 10 per cent nationally and it gives them a chance to demonstrate a depth of understanding not required by Advanced GCE. Students completing an AEA in a modern foreign language should be able to communicate confidently, clearly and accurately, using a complex and varied language. For the AEA in French, for instance, students answer a series of questions based on pieces of writing which could be either literary or non-literary. They then have to make a comparison of the pieces of writing. The examination is externally assessed and students receive either a Merit or Distinction. Those exams not making the level of Merit will receive an ungraded classification.

How is an A/AS level in a modern language taught and assessed?

To do well at A level languages you will probably need a good grade (A or B) at the language at GCSE because students need to build on what they've learned previously. Teaching is via combination of conversations in the language, written exercises, listening to the language and reading practice. Assessment is by a combination of written exams, oral exams, listening exams, reading comprehension and a small element of coursework.

Choosing other subjects to go with a modern language

You may choose to study more than one language at A level or you may wish to combine your one language with a different kind of subject. Languages go well almost anything but popular combing subjects include English Literature, History, Music, Business, Law and Mathematics.

Modern languages at HE level

This is a very popular option at HE level and you may wish to study the language on its own, in combination with literature, or the literature alone. Unless you are native speaker, in the vast majority of cases, you will need a good A level grade in the subject which you wish to pursue at university.

A degree in Modern Languages?

As well as degrees in specific languages (and literatures), many institutions offer a degree in combined Modern Languages. To get onto one of these courses, you often have to have studied two languages at A level. On the whole a degree in a Modern Language will require a very competence of the language and will be much broader in its scope than the subject at A level. Sample modules form a French degree course could include:

- Advanced French linguistics
- Cinema in France
- French: the linguist's view
- Landmarks: reading the classics of French literature
- Language, communication and society
- Textual revolutions: writing in 19th Century France.

Combining Modern Languages with other degree subjects

Studying a modern language jointly with another degree subject is a very popular option. It's quite common to see combinations with English, Politics, Maths, History, Classics, Music, Anthropology, Travel and Tourism, Management, Law and many others.

Foundation degrees and Diplomas

There are a few Foundation degrees related to modern languages. Often they are combined with specific vocational areas such as tourism. There are no BTEC Higher Nationals in Modern Languages.

Modern Languages and your future career

Non-graduate jobs

Languages are a desirable asset at any level of employment. If you want to go into work straight after A levels, you could try approaching companies who do business with foreign countries or target tourism industries such as airlines, travel agencies and tour operators. You may only start at a junior level but there isn't so much of a graduate culture in these sectors so you should be able progress quickly if you are good at your job.

Graduate jobs directly related to Modern Languages

There are a few jobs where Modern Languages are central to the job. These include translation and interpreting work, teaching Modern Languages, some areas of journalism and some areas of work within the Diplomatic Service. In many cases, however, the languages you have learned are secondary to the main skills and knowledge needed for the job. Having said that, they can often come in handy later on in your career, so it's important not to let your skills get too rusty.

Graduate jobs where a degree in Modern Languages could be useful

- **Buying/purchasing:** promotes and negotiates sales of products or services to customers worldwide.

- **Chartered accountant:** provides financial information and maintains general accounting systems and performs audits on clients often on both their UK and foreign operations.
- **Diplomatic service:** most posts abroad involve dealing with representatives of overseas governments, explaining British foreign policy and negotiating over different issues or, in some cases, promoting exports and assisting trade.
- **Distribution/logistics manager:** co-ordinates the supply, movement and storage of goods and raw materials, including operational management.
- **English as a foreign language teacher:** teaching English to foreign students in either the UK or overseas.
- **Marketing:** analysing market information and promoting products worldwide with a view to achieving optimum market share and profitability.
- **Publishing and printing:** initially you are likely to be recruited into sales, marketing, production, finance, editorial or administration. Over a third of the books published in the UK are sold overseas.
- **Solicitor:** even in the UK, solicitors' services are offered in 22 languages and many big commercial firms have offices in trading nations worldwide.

Further information

Centre for Information on Language
Teaching and Research (CILT)   www.cilt.org.uk

The Institute of Linguists   www.iol.org.uk

The Institute of Translation
and Interpreting   www.iti.org.uk

MUSIC

This subject will introduce students to a wide variety of music, particularly from the Western classical tradition and jazz, but students are also expected to do their own performing and composing and there is a considerable amount of freedom in choosing the style, genre or repertoire. In essence, this course is for those who want to develop a career in music or simply for those who want to deepen their appreciation of music. For those who choose to study Music Technology and, to a certain extent, BTEC Nationals in Media, Music and Performing Arts, the emphasis is much more on the study music through technology and how to use technology to make music effectively. It also shows students what an incredible impact technology has had on music, in particular the components of digital technology. While there is some overlap with A level Music in that students learn about musical traditions (e.g. Western classical music and jazz), the emphasis is always on how technology is used in relation to those traditions or styles. There is also a greater emphasis on analysing modern popular music.

Subject options

You can study Music at GCE A/AS level. Some schools and colleges also offer GCE A/AS level in Music and BTEC Nationals in Media, Music and Performing Arts.

A/AS level Music

For an exact definition of the AS and A2 syllabus you will be studying, you should consult your school, college or the exam board itself. Whichever exam board your school uses, it will have the following elements to the course: performance; the history of music; listening comprehension; composing; and understanding the mechanics of music. The following outline is based on the AQA specification.

Unit 1: Influences on music
The Western classical tradition; choral music in the baroque period; music theatre; British popular music (1960 to the present day).

Unit 2: Composing – creating musical ideas
Compositional techniques; free composition or pastiche in response to a given brief; arranging.

Unit 3: Performing – interpreting musical ideas
Solo and/or ensemble performances; technology-based performances.

Unit 4: Music in context
The Western classical tradition; English choral music in the 20th Century; chamber music; jazz and blues.

Unit 5: Composing – creating musical ideas

Compositional techniques; free composition or pastiche in response to a given brief; arranging.

Unit 6: Performing – a musical performance

A choice of solo, acoustic and/or technology-based performances.

AS students complete units one to three; A2 students complete all four. You will be assessed by a combination of written exams, coursework and observed performances.

A/AS level Music Technology

Edexcel is the only exam board currently offering this course. A brief outline of the syllabus is given below:

Unit 1: The development of technology in music

This module focuses on how technology has impacted music and how technology can be used to compose and perform music. Students become familiar with the language and terms of music technology and learn about specific technologies such as MIDI sequencing.

Unit 2: Music from the Western classical tradition

Students learn about the historical context of this musical tradition and how it has influenced contemporary performers and composers. This unit also explores how technology has been used to interpret music from this tradition.

Unit 3: Popular music and jazz

This module introduces students to pop and rock music as well as jazz written since the beginning of the 20th Century until the present day. Students learn about the structures of the music and the musical methods used, with particularly reference to technology.

Unit 4a: Music for the moving image

This unit is about how music has been written for TV and film as well as the musical methods and structures involved. This is done in relation to core 'texts' such as *Psycho, Titanic, Robin Hood Prince of Thieves* and *Planet of the Apes.*

Unit 4b: Words and music

This module examines the interrelationships between words and music and the historical influence on them. This is done in relation to 'core albums' such as Elton John's *Captain Fantastic and the Brown Dirt Cowboy;* Queen's *A Night at the Opera;* Peter Gabriel's *US* and Pink Floyd's *Dark Side of the Moon.*

The course also includes practical work in listening, composition and performance. As usual A2 candidates do the full syllabus whereas AS candidates do half of it.

A good grade at GCSE Music is usually required in order to study this subject at A level. Teaching is by listening to musical works, reading about the history of music, and the practical work of composing and performing. Students for this course will be using technology a lot so they should be comfortable with that. Assessment is by written examination, performance and coursework.

BTEC National

BTEC Nationals in Media, Music and Performing Arts are available in three levels (Award, Certificate and Diploma), and are offered by Edexcel exam board.

The music-related topics available at Award level (equivalent to one A level) are:

- Music (Composing)
- Music (Performing)
- Music Technology (DJ Technology)
- Music Technology (Recording).

The music-related topics available at Certificate and Diploma level (equivalent to two and three A levels) are:

- Music
- Music Technology.

Assessment for this course is by completion of a portfolio of evidence, but students must spend a certain period of working in a relevant setting.

Choosing other subjects to go with Music

Music goes well with a whole range of subjects including the Humanities, Literature, IT/Computing, Mathematics as well as more practical media or performance-related subjects.

Music at HE level

You will need A level Music to study it at a higher level. Music is usually offered as a single subject or jointly with something else. It's a subject which is not offered by every institution and increasingly universities are trying to position themselves as centres of excellence or specialist centres for Music.

A degree in Music?

Like most degrees, Music usually has an element of compulsory modules as well as some flexibility over specialist modules you can choose later on in the course. A degree in this subject will allow you to go into much greater depth than you did at A level and of course you will be able to develop even further your skills in listening, composition and performance. A typical Music could include the following modules.

Year 1:

- Historical topics 1
- Introduction to world music

- Practice and theory of performance
- Principles of tonal music
- Studies in contemporary music
- Techniques of composition.

Year 2:

- Historical topics 2
- Issues in theory & analysis
- Musical techniques 2
- Notations of Western music.

Year 3:

- Composition
- Musicology
- Special study
- Performance.

Plus options from a whole range of subjects such as Film Music, Mozart's Piano Concertos, Music, Politics, Ideology, Viennese Modernism and many more.

Combining Music with other degree subjects

Universities offer combinations depending on the structure of their own academic departments, but typical combinations include: Music with a modern foreign language; Music with Management; Drama and Music; History and Music; Mathematics and Music.

Foundation degrees and Diplomas

There are some Foundation degrees in Music-related areas, but not in 'pure' Music. There are BTEC Higher Nationals available in Music Performance and Production.

Music and your future career

Non-graduate jobs

It's hard to go into a musical career with A level Music alone but it could give you a head start in terms of showing your interest and knowledge of music. So long as you are prepared to work your way up from the bottom, it's quite possible to find junior roles within radio, a music magazine or a record company.

Graduate job directly related to Music

Even graduate jobs can be difficult to obtain because of the competitive nature of the industry and the relatively small number of openings. Jobs most closely related, either directly after graduating or after further training and work experience, comprise the following:

- **Composer:** writes original music, often commissioned by a third party. Very few musicians derive all their income from composition: an average income from composition would be 20 per cent with the 80 per cent usually made up from teaching or performing.
- **Editorial assistant:** assists in the production of manuscripts and textbooks for music teaching. All the music publishers in the UK are small employers recruiting music graduates only occasionally and expecting them to start at the very bottom.
- **Magazine journalist:** there are many specialist publications covering all aspects of music. However, the field is extremely competitive and it may be necessary to work freelance, and undertake training in journalism.
- **Musician:** most musicians are self-employed and accept a wide range of engagements. These can include not only orchestral, ensemble or solo work in the classical field but also in clubs, cruise liners and cabaret in the popular music area.
- **Music librarian:** responsible for the acquisition and promotion of library music resources within the community, in education, or within a private company. Graduates need to qualify as a professional librarian first before being able to specialise in a field such as music.
- **Music therapist:** using music to treat, educate or rehabilitate people with emotional, physical or mental problems based in hospitals, schools, prisons, etc.
- **Private music teacher:** involved in the teaching of music in schools for all ages, both in the state and independent sectors. Some are employed as peripatetic teachers working in a number of schools in an area and are employed by the music service of LEAs.

Graduate jobs where a degree in Music could be useful

- **Community arts worker:** concerned with the promotion of the arts in the community often through working with young people out of school hours.
- **Film/video production manager:** working on programmes in radio, television or for video production and post-production. This is very popular, but difficult to break into even if you are prepared to start at the bottom.
- **Museum/art gallery curator:** there are occasional openings for curators and assistants of musical collections in the major museums following the appropriate postgraduate training.
- **Musical performance/festival organiser:** is employed on a small scale by orchestras, opera or ballet companies and concert halls. Can also be employed by companies, conference centres and arenas to host and organise big music festivals such as Glastonbury, the Reading Music Festival and many others.

Further information

The British Society for Music Therapy	www.bsmt.org
The Royal Academy of Music	www.ram.ac.uk

T. Delles, *The British and International Music Yearbook* (Rhinegold Publishing, 2008)

PERFORMING ARTS

Post-16 courses on offer in Performing Arts are of a practical nature. They give students a thorough insight into the performing arts sector and equipping them with the skills and knowledge needed to enter into the many different employment areas in the field and/or to apply for courses in Higher Education in this area. The aspects of the performing arts industry that students can learn about include: dance; drama; music; music technology; arts administration and marketing; technical and production aspects of performance.

Subject options

This subject is available as an Applied GCE A/AS level and students might also be interested in BTEC Nationals in Media, Music and Performing Arts. (A/AS level Dance is offered through one exam board, but currently it's not offered by a large number of schools and colleges.)

A/AS level

The outline below relates to the syllabus set out in the OCR guidelines. There will be some variation in relation to different exam boards but the same content is more or less covered.

Unit no.	Unit title
1	Investigating performing arts organisations *(e.g. cinemas, theatres, dance halls, stage schools, etc. and the different job functions that exist within them.)*
2	Professional practice: skills development *Students produce a skills development plan for either performance (e.g. dance, acting, music, etc.) or production (e.g. lighting, make-up, arts administration, etc.)*
3	Professional practice: performance *Students put into practice the skills that they have learned by conducting a performance for a group.*
4	Professional practice: production *Students put into practice the skills that learned by putting on a production.*
5	Getting work *An introduction to the different careers and further study within the sector and the main skills needed to succeed in the field.*
6	Exploring repertoire *Students from both the production and performance pathways get together to produce a piece of drama.*
7	Producing your showcase *A synoptic module whereby students can show all the skills they've developed over the course.*
8	Production demonstration *Students produce a piece of work in response to a brief set by the teacher.*

You need no prior knowledge of this subject to take the course, however, and interest in the topic as well as career motivation in this area are advantages. As well as classroom work, students may visit different types of arts-related organisations, and do lots of independent research about the sector. Assessment is by a combination of externally assessment and internally assessed portfolios of evidence.

BTEC Nationals

BTEC Nationals in Media, Music and Performing Arts are available in three levels (Award, Certificate and Diploma), and are offered by Edexcel exam board:

The performing arts-related topics available at Award level (equivalent to one A level) are:

- Performing Arts (Acting)
- Performing Arts (Dance)
- Performing Arts (Musical Theatre)
- Performing Arts (Physical Theatre).

The performing arts-related topics available at Certificate level (equivalent to two A levels) are:

- Performing Arts
- Performing Arts (Acting)
- Performing Arts (Dance)
- Performing Arts (Musical Theatre).

The performing arts-related topics available at Diploma level (equivalent to three A levels) are:

- Performing Arts
- Performing Arts (Acting)
- Performing Arts (Dance)
- Performing Arts (Musical Theatre).

Assessment for this course is by completion of a portfolio of evidence, but students must spend a certain period of working in a relevant setting.

Choosing other subjects to go with Performing Arts

Subjects that go well with this one include English, Media, Music Technology as well as many others.

Performing Arts at HE level

There are a few courses available at degree level covering many aspects of performing arts, but the majority tend to specialise in one or two areas. Decide which part of performing arts you excel in and go for that. This is also a popular subject at Foundation degree level.

A degree in Performing Arts?

There are a few degrees that cover the broad subject of performing arts as a single degree without specialising in one particular area. Some of the areas that such degrees cover include:

- Arts in the community
- Dance in education
- Film, text performance
- International theatre since 1945
- Music in education
- Performing arts: contemporary practice
- Performance in virtual worlds
- Storytelling and poetry in performance
- The film industry – School of Arts and Humanities.

Combining Performing Arts with other degree subjects

This subject goes well with Music, a modern language, English, IT/Computing, Media and countless others.

Foundation degrees and Diplomas

BTEC Higher Nationals exist in Media, Music and Performing Arts. There are also a number of Foundation degree courses in many different aspects of performing arts. You can search for them at www.ucas.com.

Performing Arts and your future career

Non-graduate jobs

If you want a career in performance or in the technical side of performing arts, you will probably have to go and do further study. It's possible to get your foot in the door straight after A levels though by working in an administrative role within a theatre or opera house within the box office, for instance.

Graduate jobs directly related to Performing Arts

Some related jobs will require relevant postgraduate study and if you want to become a performer you may need further professional training.

- **Actor:** using speech, body language and movement, an actor communicates a character and situations to an audience.
- **Dancer:** working in a variety of genres, from classical ballet and West End musicals to contemporary dance and freestyle (disco), a dancer's role may also involve education or therapy, as well as entertainment.
- **Primary school teacher:** teaching younger children the full range of curriculum subjects.

- **Secondary school teacher:** teaching drama, music or other curriculum subjects in schools and colleges.

Graduate jobs where a degree in Performing Arts could be useful

- **Arts administrator:** facilitates the planning and promotion of visual and performing arts activities, sometimes specialising in areas such as finance and marketing.
- **Community arts worker:** concerned with the promotion of the arts in the community often through working with young people in schools and youth centres.
- **Drama therapist:** using drama to treat or educate people with health or emotional difficulties through therapeutic techniques.
- **Editorial assistant:** music degrees may enable entry to specialist fields concerning manuscripts or new music.
- **Journalist:** there are many specialist publications covering the arts but entry is very competitive. Graduates could start in mainstream broadcast or print journalism and specialise or become freelance later.
- **Programme researcher:** supports the producer by helping to organise and plan the programme.
- **Television production assistant:** organises and co-ordinates programme activities, booking performers and facilities and providing administrative support.

Further information

Council for Dance Education and Training	www.cdet.org.uk
Incorporated Society of Musicians	www.ism.org
National Council for Drama Training	www.ncdt.co.uk

PHILOSOPHY

Philosophy literally means 'the love of wisdom'. The discipline of philosophy has been around for a very long time, as far back as the Greeks and remains popular today. The kinds of wisdom that is studied varies enormously but in general includes questions about the meaning of life, the nature of reality, consciousness, how to live a good life, questions of ethics and much more.

Questions that philosophers could ask include:

- Do we really exist?
- Why are there wars?
- If we are controlled by genes and DNA, are we responsible for our choices?
- Can discrimination ever be justified?

The successful study of Philosophy requires an analytical, logical mind, a curiosity about the world, and the ability to look at things from different points of view.

Subject options

This subject is available at GCE A/AS level.

For an exact definition of the AS and A2 syllabus you will be studying, you should consult your school, college or the exam board itself. The main variations in Philosophy are in terms of the particular philosophers and 'strands' of Philosophy that a school chooses students to study. However, most exam boards stipulate that students should gain an appreciation of the major elements of philosophical thought.

Main elements of the course

A broad outline of a Philosophy A level syllabus could look like the following:

Unit 1: An introduction to philosophy (1)
Reason and experience; why should I be governed?; why should I be moral?

Unit 2: An introduction to philosophy (2)
Knowledge of the external world; tolerance; the value of art; God and the world; free will vs. determinism.

Unit 3: Key themes in philosophy
Philosophy of mind; political philosophy; epistemology and metaphysics; moral philosophy; philosophy of religion.

Unit 4: Philosophical problems
Hume; Plato; Mill; Descartes; Nietzsche.

How is A/AS level Philosophy taught and assessed?

Philosophy is taught by a mixture of students' independent learning and classroom work. To get the very top grades, students are encouraged to read around the subject to support the knowledge they gain in class. Class lessons may also include the discussion of philosophical concepts. As with some other subjects, the volume of reading and writing is high in this subject and students should be prepared for that before they embark on subject. Furthermore, becoming familiar with Philosophical concepts and terms can be difficult at first.

Assessment is usually by written answers to questions in an exam. AS students complete units one and two; A2 students complete one to four.

Choosing other subjects to go with Philosophy

Philosophy is an interesting subject because it touches on science, law, religion, history, literature, mathematics as well as politics. In this sense, many subjects could be good to have as a combination. This subject would be widely accepted as one of the supporting A levels for entry onto most degree courses, unless a particular course required all science or maths-related subjects.

Philosophy at HE level

It's not necessary to have an A level in Philosophy to study it at a higher level. This is partly because the subject is not widely available as subject choice through schools and colleges.

A degree in Philosophy?

Although most university Philosophy courses include (usually in the first year) an introduction to the main strands of the discipline, the content can vary widely. Some will focus on more traditional forms of philosophy such as Plato and Aristotle; others will place their emphasis on applying philosophy to contemporary issues in politics, law, religion and society in general.

Possible options outside core modules could include the study of particular philosophers such as Wittgenstein or Hegel; the study of philosophy by country of origin such as Indian Philosophy and Greek Philosophy; or the study of certain 'schools' of philosophy such Marxism (named after Karl Marx) and Aesthetics (the study and appreciation of beauty and art).

Combining Philosophy with other degree subjects

Because the study of Philosophy cuts across so many other disciplines, it is quite common to see this subject being combined with both arts and sciences. A very well-known combination or joint degree is Politics, Philosophy and Economics (PPE) offered by some universities. However, combinations with History, Modern Languages, Theology, Mathematics, Physics, Literature and Classics are pretty common too.

Foundation degrees and Diplomas

Given that Philosophy is not a vocational subject, there aren't any specific Diplomas or Foundation degrees in it.

Philosophy and your future career

Non-graduate jobs

Philosophy is not a vocational subject and therefore it will not lead directly to a particular career. Undoubtedly, it does develop some very useful skills such as critical thinking, the ability to create a persuasive argument, independent thinking, good judgement and logic. These could be useful for a range of jobs such as administration, some government work, and some junior aspects of managerial work.

Graduate jobs where Philosophy could be useful

Careers include those which, while open to graduates of any discipline, require strong analytical and communication skills:

- **Advertising account planner:** analyses consumer response to advertisements and helps to integrate this into advertising strategy; evaluates the effectiveness of advertising.
- **Civil Service administrator/local government administrator:** assists in the formulation of policies and procedures, in a government department or local authority, and co-ordinates their implementation.
- **Information technology consultant:** gives independent advice to clients on IT solutions to business problems; analyses problems, makes recommendations and develops and implements new systems.
- **Marketing executive, consumer products**: assists in the development of brands and the promotion of fast moving consumer goods (FMCG) and products to the public.
- **Newspaper journalist:** reports on news and other items of current interest for newspapers.
- **Personnel officer:** advises on all policies relating to human resources in an organisation, including employee planning, recruitment, pay and conditions of work, training, and welfare.
- **Political party research officer:** employed in a variety of settings, including Higher Education, political parties and independent agencies. Includes working for members of Parliament and members of European Parliament.
- **Public affairs consultant (lobbyist):** represents the clients' case to those in government who make decisions that affect them. The client may be a large company, a trade association, a pressure group or a local authority.
- **Publishing copy/sub-editor**: ensures that a manuscript is accurate, appropriate for intended readership, has a consistent style and a logical structure for the publisher before it goes to the production stage.

- **Solicitor:** advises individuals and organisations on legal problems; prepares wills, contracts and other legal documents; researches and advises on points of law.
- **TV programme researcher:** generates programme ideas, researches background material, briefs production teams and presenters.

Further information

The Royal Institute of Philosophy   www.royalinstitutephilosophy.org

T. Nagel, *What does it all mean?* (OUP, 2004)

B. Russell, *The Problems of Philosophy* (OUP, 2001)

PHYSICAL EDUCATION (PE)

A level PE develops students' knowledge, understanding and skills in many areas. Firstly, as an A level PE student you would learn about specific physical activities and sports and develop the skills of planning, performing and evaluating these activities. But you would also get an insight into the historical and social context of sport as well the relationship between psychology and physiology in sport. This is both an academic and a practical subject! If you choose to study a more practical course, such as a BTEC National, then the emphasis will be much more on the Sports industry and the possible career pathways within it.

Subject options

This subject is available as GCE A/AS level in Physical Education. BTEC Nationals are also available in Sport. From 2010, you will also be able to study an Advanced Diploma in Sport and Leisure.

A/AS level

For an exact definition of the AS and A2 syllabus you will be studying, you should consult your school, college or the exam board itself. The following outline is roughly based on the Edexcel syllabus.

The social basis of sport and recreation

This unit seeks to investigate the historical and cultural basis of sport in order to develop an understanding of the current role and provision that sport maintains in modern society. The unit also includes an investigation into the social factors that influence both performance and participation.

Enhancing performance

Students carry out a number of activities or sports and learn how to improve in these areas as well as how to measure the improvement.

Exercise and training

The unit will advance students' understanding of anatomy and physiology attained at KS4 and build on this through the principles and methods of training.

Global trends in international sport

Students undertake a comparative investigation of sport and recreation in a number of differing regions. These have been grouped together in broad geographical groups. The requirement is to identify trends and systems in similar countries.

Refining performance

This builds on previous units of enhancing performance and exercise and training.

Scientific principles of exercise and performance

This unit advances the students' knowledge of exercise and training, and provides an introduction to energy systems, sports psychology and mechanics.

AS level students 50 per cent of the course whereas A2 students complete all of it.

By its very nature, PE is not a classroom-bound subject. There will be the usual classroom note-taking but you will also spend much time engaging in various types of physical activities, games and sports. Assessment is by a combination of written exams, coursework and assessed practical activities.

BTEC Nationals

BTEC Nationals in Sport are available in three levels (Award, Certificate and Diploma), and are offered by Edexcel exam board.

The sport-related topics available at Award level (equivalent to one A level) are:

- Sport
- Sport and Exercise Sciences
- Sport (Performance and Excellence).

The sport-related topics available at Certificate and Diploma level (equivalent to two and three A levels) are:

- Sport (Development, Coaching and Fitness)
- Sport and Exercise Sciences
- Sport (Outdoor Adventure)
- Sport (Performance and Excellence).

Assessment for this course is by completion of a portfolio of evidence, but students must spend a certain period of working in a relevant setting if relevant.

Choosing other A level subjects to go with Sports Science PE

Subjects that may go well with PE include Leisure Studies, Computing/ICT, Biology and Psychology. If you want to study Sports Science at degree level, you may want to choose two Sciences to go along with PE.

Sport Science at HE level

There are courses in PE at a Higher Education level but they are often linked with teacher training courses because PE is still seen to some extent as a school subject. It is more common now to have HE courses in Sports Science. Institutions sometimes express a preference for Sciences at A level rather than PE, so always check in advance!

A degree in PE/Sports Science?

A degree in this subject will explore the area in greater depth and breadth while offering you some options to specialise. A sample of degree modules could look like the following:

- Fitness and training
- IT for sport and exercise science
- Nutrition
- Physiology of exercise and health
- Sociology of sport
- Sport and exercise pedagogy
- Structural kinesiology.

Combining PE/Sports Science with other degree subjects

This can be combined with almost any other, depending on your preferences and the flexibility of academic departments. Common combinations include:

- Chemistry and Sports Science
- English and Sports Science
- Geography and Sports Science
- Mathematics and Sports Science
- Physics and Sports Science
- Sports Science with Management.

Foundation degrees and Diplomas

Edexcel offers BTEC Higher Nationals in Sport there are many Foundation Courses available related to Sports studies and Sports Science. Visit www.ucas.com to search for these.

PE/Sports Science and your future career

Non-graduate jobs

It's possible to get into a few sports related areas without a degree. These include junior positions in sports clubs and gyms, as well as administrative roles within a hotel and leisure complex. It's even possible to become a personal trainer/coach with some further training, although not necessarily at degree level. Of course, other non-sports jobs are open to you too.

Graduate jobs directly related to PE/Sports Science

- **Fitness centre manager:** employed mainly in commercial health clubs and gymnasia to manage the provision of physical fitness and lifestyle programmes.
- **Leisure centre manager:** there are opportunities in both the public and private sectors for promoting and running leisure and recreation centres.

- **Lifestyle consultant:** employed mainly in the private sector to provide physical fitness instruction and prescription of exercise/fitness programmes for individuals.
- **Outdoor pursuits manager:** manages a centre offering instruction to a wide range of people in outdoor activities.
- **Secondary school teacher or Higher Education lecturer:** there are opportunities for teaching PE in tertiary and FE colleges as well as maintained and independent schools. Lecturing in HE is also available.
- **Sports administrator:** works within a governing body or the Sports Council. The role may be similar to that of the sports development officer (see below) but it is likely to have a greater emphasis on administrative and financial aspects.
- **Sports coach/instructor:** here are a few full-time posts in some sports. This work can also form part of the work of a sports development officer or a recreation assistant in a sports centre.
- **Sports development officer:** promotes various sports within the community, usually amongst particular target groups, or develops one sport on behalf of a local authority, governing body or professional association.
- **Sports therapist:** mainly concerned with the prevention and treatment of injury in sport and with improving and maintaining physical performance.

Graduate jobs where a degree in PE/Sports Science could be useful

- **Armed forces:** the active nature of many of the jobs and the leadership role of officers can suit sports people.
- **Health promotion specialist:** understanding of nutrition and the relation of fitness to health is useful background for a health promotion specialist.
- **Journalism:** familiarity with sports is obviously an asset if you want to be a journalist specialising in reporting and writing about sport.
- **Marketing:** the sports equipment and leisure wear industries could well value your knowledge of sport and exercise.
- **Physiotherapist:** this would be good preparation for a career in sports therapy but the training would take at least two further years after your degree.
- **Police officer:** this challenging job could suit sports management/science graduates for reasons similar to those given for the armed services.

Further information

The British Association of Sport and
Exercise Sciences (BASES)   www.bases.org.uk

Sport England   www.sportengland.org

UK Sport   www.uksport.gov.uk

PHYSICS

The study of physics will encourage you to understand how the physical world works, and will prove useful if you are considering a career in engineering, electronics, computing and many others. This course will help you establish links between theory and experiment, and will also help you:

- learn how scientific work is evaluated, published and verified by the scientific community
- gain an understanding of how physics has changed over time and is used in the modern world
- explore the properties of motion, nuclear physics, energy transfer and electricity
- develop a better awareness of how advances in science and technology affect the world.

Subject options

This subject is available as a GCE A/AS level and also as an Advanced Extension Award (AEA). If you're interested in the Electronics element of Physics, some schools offer an A/AS level purely in this subject.

A/AS level

For an exact definition of the AS and A2 syllabus you will be studying, you should consult your school, college or the exam board itself. The following outline is roughly based on the Edexcel syllabus.

Unit 1: Mechanics and radioactivity

Forces, vectors and motion; graphs, energy, power and efficiency; Newton's laws, moments and couples; momentum and impulse; radioactivity – types and detection; radioactivity – the nucleus; atomic and sub-atomic scattering.

Unit 2: Electricity and thermal physics

Electrical properties; more advanced concepts; applied heat; the gas laws; kinetic theory; an introduction to thermodynamics; heat engines.

Unit 3: Topics

Students can choose one of the following four to study:

- Astrophysics
- Medical physics
- Nuclear and particle physics
- Solid materials.

Unit 4: Waves and our Universe

Motion in a circle; simple harmonic motion, (SHM); waves and interference; light (1); light (2); introduction to quantum physics; atomic models; Doppler, the red shift and the creation of time.

Unit 5: Fields and Forces

Electrical fields (1); electrical fields (2); gravity fields; magnetic fields; introduction to capacitance; inductance (1); inductance (2).

Unit 6: Synthesis

This is a synoptic module where students draw on all the knowledge gained from the different module so far.

AS students complete modules one to three, A2 students complete all six modules.

Advanced Extension Award

The AEA in Physics, aimed at the top 10 per cent of students, will assess the ability to solve a range of unfamiliar problems, problems that can be solved from students' knowledge gained at A level. Students answer a series of questions in examination conditions and will be assessed on the extent to which they can apply and communicate their understanding of physics (e.g. problem-solving and deductive reasoning; critical analysis; evaluation and synthesis).

For more details of specification and marking criteria, visit the CCEA website (www.rewardinglearning.co.uk).

How is A/AS level Physics taught and assessed?

Students will need a GCSE in Physics to enroll in this subject unless they have very good grades in Maths and related subjects like design and technology. There is a lot of classroom work as well as practical work in the lab, carrying out experiments. Assessment is by a combination of written exams and assessed practical work. There is usually no coursework component in A level Physics so think twice before choosing this subject if exams are not your strength!

Choosing other subjects to go with Physics

There is a lot of Maths involved in A level Physics, so studying Maths at A level too is a big help, and more often than not you will need Maths A level to study Physics at degree level. Other subjects that go well with Physics include Engineering, Design and Technology, Chemistry and IT/Computing.

Physics at HE level

Physics at degree level has been around for a very long time and is well established in many universities. Students usually have the option of studying specific types of Physics (e.g. Astrophysics) or they can choose courses such as applied Physics of Pure Physics.

A degree in Physics?

Most Physics degrees have compulsory options in the first and second years with some flexibility later on. Modules on a Physics course could include:

- Astrophysics
- Computational physics
- Classical mechanics and special relativity
- Electromagnetism
- Introductory quantum mechanics
- Introduction to plasma physics
- Nuclear physics
- Radiation physics
- Statistical mechanics.

Combining Physics with other degree subjects

Popular combinations include: Physics and Maths; Physics and Management; Physics and Computer Science; Physics and Philosophy as well as others.

Foundation degrees and Diplomas

BTEC Higher Nationals are available in applied Science and there are one or two Foundation degrees available in Physics. Search at www.ucas.com.

Physics and your future career

Non-graduate jobs

To work in Physics straight after A levels is a bit difficult as most jobs in this field involve further study. A job as a trainee lab technician is possible. In terms of non-science jobs, there will be opportunities in the commercial sector so long as you demonstrate the skills you've developed from the course which includes problem-solving, numeracy, manual dexterity and logical thinking.

Graduate jobs directly related to Physics

- **Electronics engineer:** develops and designs an electronic product, process or device from the initial brief through a tested prototype up to manufacture.
- **Geoscientist:** collects, analyses and appraises physical data about the earth in order to discover commercially exploitable mineral and hydrocarbon reserves.
- **Materials engineer:** works on the manufacture, development and use of a wide range of materials, e.g. glass and ceramics, metals, polymers.

- **Medical physicist:** provides scientific support to medical staff in the accurate, effective and safe diagnosis and treatment of patients.
- **Meteorologist:** interprets observations from the land surface, oceans and from the upper atmosphere to forecast weather both short and long-term, e.g. the results of global warming.
- **Research scientist**: organises and carries out systematic investigations into physical properties, behaviour and phenomena with the aim of introducing, developing or improving products or processes.
- **Scientific laboratory technician:** assists scientists and others who are engaged in research, development, analysis or scientific investigations by carrying out a variety of technical and experimental tasks.
- **Secondary school teacher:** teaches physics and/or balanced science. A PGCE is necessary for teaching posts in state schools.

Graduate jobs where a degree in Physics could be useful

- **Forensic scientist:** investigates scientific aspects of crime, fires and accidents.
- **Scientific journalist:** researches, writes and edits scientific news articles and features.
- **Systems analyst:** analyses the requirements of systems in both a business and technical context and determines the optimum solutions.
- **Technical author:** designs and writes documentation which communicates technical information.
- **Technical sales engineer:** provides the major link between the company producing technical goods and services and its customers, negotiating sales, orders, price and quality.

Further information

Institute of Physics   www.iop.org

Physics and Astronomy online reference   www.physlink.com

T. Duncan *Advanced Physics*
(Hodder Murray, 2008)

PSYCHOLOGY

The study of psychology will help you understand your own behaviour as well as that of other people. The course also looks at topical issues, such as stress, eyewitness testimony and eating disorders that can be better understood and managed using psychological methods. A level Psychology will also help you learn about various different types of research methods and how to present results and theories as well as giving you an understanding of how knowledge of psychology can be useful in everyday life. Students of this course develop the ability to critically analyse the nature and source of psychological theories and find out how to design and report psychological investigations and to interpret their results.

Subject options

This subject is available as GCE A/AS and, for the top 10 per cent of candidates, as an Advanced Extension Award.

A/AS level

For an exact definition of the AS and A2 syllabus you will be studying, you should consult your school, college or the exam board itself. The following outline is roughly based on the AQA specification.

Unit 1: Cognitive and developmental psychology; research methods
Cognitive psychology, including memory and eyewitness testimony; developmental psychology, including early social development, attachment and the effects of everyday care; research methods, in the context of the topic areas.

Unit 2: Biological psychology, social psychology and individual differences
Biological psychology, including stress, factors affecting stress, managing stress; social psychology, including majority and minority influence, obedience and independent behaviour; individual differences; including definitions of abnormality, approaches and therapies.

Unit 3: Topics in psychology
Biological rhythms and sleep; perception; relationships; aggression; eating behaviour; gender; intelligence and learning; cognition and development.

Unit 4: Psychopathology, psychology in action and research methods
Biological approaches; behaviourism; social learning theory; cognitive; psychodynamic and humanistic approaches; comparison of approaches; debates in psychology; methods in psychology; inferential statistics; issues in research.

Advanced Extension Award

The AEA in Psychology, aimed at the top 10 per cent of students, will assess the ability to answer previously unseen questions on a range of issues in psychology. Students answer the questions in examination conditions (usually three hours long) and will be assessed on the extent to which they can apply and communicate their understanding of psychology and use key skills (e.g. reasoning; critical analysis; evaluation and synthesis). You will have to draw on all you've learned from the A level course and be able to comment on key debates in Psychology and show a breadth of understanding of the subject.

For more details of specification and marking criteria, visit the AQA website (www.aqa. org.uk).

How is A/AS level Psychology taught and assessed?

There is no need to have any prior knowledge of this subject to take it at A/AS level. All you need is an interest in how the human mind and behaviour works and at least a semi-scientific mind. There is a lot of classroom work note-taking about theories but also some practical experiments are carried out. You also spend a long time learning how to carry out a psychological experiment and research effectively and correctly. Assessment is by written paper, although some courses may have an assessed project/practical element. A2 candidates complete units one and two; A2 candidates do all four.

Choosing other subjects to go with Psychology

If you want to do a degree in Psychology then it doesn't usually matter which subjects you do alongside it. However, some universities may prefer you to have studied the Sciences, or at least Biology. That said, Psychology also goes well with subjects such as Law, English, Philosophy and Business Studies.

Psychology at HE level

Psychology is offered at very many universities and colleges. Like many subjects, it's possible to specialise in a type of Psychology such as Development Psychology. What is important is that, if you want to be a professional psychologist later on, your undergraduate degree must be accredited by the British Psychological Society (BPS).

A degree in Psychology?

As with most courses, there are some core modules and some optional ones. Some sample modules of a university degree course might include:

- Biological psychology
- Cognitive neuroscience
- Psychology of religion

- Sensation and perception
- Statistical methods.

Combing Psychology with other degree subjects

Subjects often studied alongside Psychology include Maths, Computing/IT, Philosophy, Physics, English and Religious Studies.

Foundation degrees and Diplomas

There a few Psychology-related Foundation degrees available but they are usually focusing on one particular area, such as Psychology and Crime. Some students may be interested in the BTEC Higher Nationals in applied Science or Health and Care which have some overlap with Psychology.

Psychology and your future career

Non-graduate jobs

Psychology gives you many useful skills such as the ability to research, analyse data, think logically and communicate effectively. These skills will be sought after in most sectors including Health, Business and other areas of the public sector. If you want to work in Psychology, then further study is usually required.

Graduate jobs directly related to Psychology

For all the following careers except counselling, teaching and HE lecturing, a first degree in psychology or alternative graduate conversion qualification, accredited by the British Psychological Society (BPS), is essential in order to enter further training and work.

- **Clinical psychologist:** applies psychology to the assessment and treatment of patients and clients in health care settings and conducts research in mental and physical illness.
- **Counsellor:** helps people solve problems, cope with distress and improve wellbeing. Works with clients of all ages and in a variety of settings, including health, education and the workplace.
- **Educational psychologist:** applies psychology to the learning difficulties of children and young people and advises parents, teachers and schools.
- **Forensic psychologist:** applies psychology to criminological and legal issues including the assessment and treatment of offenders, and may have trained in criminological or clinical psychology.
- **Health psychologist:** applies knowledge and understanding of behaviour to finding ways of improving the quality of health care and the standard of health in the general population.
- **Higher education lecturer:** involved in teaching psychology in colleges and Higher Education institutions.

- **Occupational psychologist:** applies psychology to people at work and organisations including selection and assessment, training, work design and organisational change.

Graduate jobs where a degree in Psychology could be useful

- **Market research executive:** provides systematically acquired information on what people buy, want, do or think and explores the reasons why.
- **Personnel officer:** advises on and implements policies relating to the use of human resources including employee planning, recruitment, training and welfare.
- **School teacher:** for secondary, teaching social science, science or appropriate national curriculum subject.
- **Social researcher:** analyses the impact and expenditure implications of proposed policy changes and monitors the effects of change.
- **Social worker:** assists and advises clients with social problems. Also specialisation as psychiatric social worker.
- **Speech and language therapist:** assesses, diagnoses and treats adults and children who suffer from disorders of voice, speech or language.
- **Psychotherapist:** develops a skilled relationship with clients in order to explore the underlying causes of their emotional conflicts or behavioural difficulties.

Further information

The British Psychological Society   www.bps.org.uk

R. Gross, *The Psychology of Mind and Behaviour* (Hodder Arnold, 2005)

RELIGIOUS STUDIES

You don't have to belong to a particular religion to study this subject. Religious Studies allows students to consider the fundamental questions of human existence, examining issues such as the interaction between religion and science, as well as exploring religious experience and philosophical aspects of religious belief. In addition, you will be able to practise textual criticism skills developed by studying the New Testament. You will also get a better understanding of world religions.

Subject options

This subject is available at GCE A/AS level and as an Advanced Extension Award. Some students might also be interested in A/AS level Biblical Hebrew, offered by OCR.

A/AS level

All the exam boards offer this subject and the content is very similar among all of them. The following outline is based largely on the new OCR specification.

- Buddhism
- Developments in Christian theology
- Hinduism
- Islam
- Jewish scriptures
- Judaism
- New Testament
- Philosophy of religion
- Religious ethics.

Students going for AS only take two units in the above areas; A2 students complete four modules.

Advanced Extension Award

For the AEA in Religious Studies, students answer a series of questions in examination conditions and will be assessed on the extent to which they can apply their understanding of Religious Studies in a variety of contexts. In the exam, students read a series of passages, some excerpts from religious texts, answer a series of questions based on them. The AEA is aimed at the top 10 per cent of students.

How is A/AS level Religious Studies taught and assessed?

Teaching is mainly classroom based learning and discussion but there may be visits to sites of religious interest. Assessment is by a combination of written exams and possibly coursework or an extended essay.

Choosing other subjects to go with Religious Studies?

A levels that go well with this subject include English Literature, History, Psychology, Philosophy and Latin or Greek.

Religious Studies at HE level

There are many opportunities to study this subject at a higher level and a degree in this subject could be called Religious Studies, Theology or Divinity.

A degree in Religious Studies

A degree in this subject would go into much more depth than at A level, as well as being much broader in its scope in the kind of religions and religious sects studied. A sample of units that you might study during a degree programme includes:

- Does God exist?
- Islam's beginnings
- Islamic mysticism
- Jewish thought and practice
- Moral theory and religion
- Religion and the enlightenment
- The anthropology of religion
- Theories of religion
- The problem of evil.

Combining Religious Studies with other degree subjects

This subject could be combined with most Humanities subjects and common combinations include Theology and Religious Studies, History and Religious Studies, English Literature and Religious Studies and Classics and Religious Studies.

Foundation degrees and Diplomas

There are some Foundation courses related to Religious Studies but they tend to be aiming for a specific vocation, i.e. Religious Studies and Ministry.

Religious Studies and your future career

Non-graduate jobs

This is a sound A level that will enable you, along with your other subjects, to get junior positions in many areas of business, the public sector and the not-for-profit sector. Jobs in Religious Studies would be hard to find without a degree but getting an administrative position in a religious-based Non-Governmental Organisation (NGO) would be a possibility.

Graduate jobs directly related to Religious Studies

The most directly related job is a Minister of Religion who teaches the religious beliefs specific to the faith, ministering to the spiritual and social needs of people in the local community. Information is usually available through the minister of your church or religious organisation. Other related jobs include:

- **Adult education lecturer/tutor:** plans and provides a programme of learning activities for adults of all ages, backgrounds and academic levels, in line with the tutor's own expertise.
- **Higher education lecturer:** involves teaching (undergraduate and postgraduate students), research (which may include work for agencies outside the university) and administration.
- **Secondary school teacher:** involves teaching religious studies and theology in schools or colleges.

Graduate jobs where a degree in Religious Studies could be useful

- **Charity officer:** promotes the work of the charity being responsible for fundraising, arrange recruitment, training and supervision of paid and voluntary staff, devise and manage the administrative systems, including the accounts.
- **Counsellor:** concerned with counselling people with personal problems. Helps the client to explore, discover and clarify more effective ways of living.
- **Housing adviser:** offers advice and support to people who have housing difficulties.
- **Journalist:** researches and writes features for broadcasting on television or radio, or publishing in periodicals and newspapers. As a theology student you might be interested in the specialist field of religious publications.

Further information

The Buddhist Society   www.thebuddhistsociety.org.uk

Council of Christians and Jews   www.ccj.org.uk

Hinduism   www.comparative-religion.com/hinduism

Islamic Foundation   www.islamic-foundation.org.uk

National Society for Promoting
Religious Education   www.natsoc.org.uk

T. P. Burke, *The Major Religions:
An Introduction with Texts* (Wiley Blackwell, 2004)

SCIENCE (APPLIED)

Applied Science is for students who want to learn about how Science is applied in real, practical ways. This may be in commerce, in industry, in research or any other way that is practical or that affects peoples' lives. It is also for students who want to pursue specific scientific careers such as laboratory work. This subject will also develop your skills in IT, numeracy, logical thinking and problem-solving.

A/AS level Science and Society

This subject allows students to learn about science and how it affects our lives and the society in which we live. The following is based on the AQA specification:

Subject options

This subject is available as an applied GCE A/AS level. Schools might also offer GCE A/AS level Science and Society and BTEC Nationals in Science.

Unit 1: Exploring issues (1)
Theories of disease, infectious diseases, public health issues; medicines, ethics and reproductive choices; lifestyle, transport choices and fuel issues; the planet earth and the solar system; the human race, evolution and society.

Unit 2: Reading and research
A critical account of scientific reading; the study of a topical scientific issue.

Unit 3: Exploring issues (2)
Cells, chemicals and the mind; nature and nurture; how the brain works; climate change; energy supplies; sustainability.

Unit 4: Case study
Students have to evaluate a scientific or technological issue.

AS students complete units one and two; A2 students complete all four. Assessment is by a mixture of coursework and exams.

Applied A/AS level

The exam boards offer this subject covering very similar content. This subject is available in four ways: AS single award (three units); AS double award (six units); A level single award (six units) and A level double award (twelve units).

Unit no.	Unit title	Unit no.	Unit title
1	Investigating science at work	9	Sports science
2	Energy transfer systems	10	Physics of performance effects
3	Finding out about substances	11	Controlling chemical processes
4	Food science and technology	12	The actions and development of medicines
5	Choosing and using materials	13	Colour chemistry
6	Synthesising organic compounds	14	The healthy body
7	Planning and carrying out a scientific investigation	15	The role of the pathology service
8	Medical physics	16	Ecology, conservation and recycling

Students need to have reached a good standard of at least one GCSE Science subject before taking this. There is a lot of lab work, calculations and practical tasks. Sometimes visits are arranged to places of scientific interest (e.g. a chemical plant). Assessment is by a combination of written exams and portfolio of evidence.

BTEC Nationals

These qualifications are aimed to give students the practical skills needed by the job market in that particular sector. BTEC Nationals are available in three levels (Award, Certificate and Diploma):

The science subjects available at BTEC National Award level (equivalent to one A level) are:

- Applied Science (Applied Biology)
- Applied Science (Applied Chemistry)
- Applied Science (Applied Physics)
- Applied Science (Environmental Science)
- Applied Science (Forensic Science)
- Applied Science (Medical Science).

Science subjects available at BTEC National Certificate and Diploma level (equivalent to two and three A levels):

- Applied Science (Forensic Science)
- Applied Science (Laboratory and Industrial Science)
- Applied Science (Medical Science).

Assessment is by a combination of coursework, projects, case studies and examinations.

Choosing other subjects to go with Applied Science

Other Science subjects at would obviously go well but ensure there is not too much overlap – university admissions may not recognise your subjects as separate and therefore your points tally would be lower. Other subjects that might go well include Business, Environmental Science, Computing/IT and Maths. If you want to study a particular Science at university, you should study that subject at A level.

Science at HE level?

There are some science-based degree courses for which A level Science would count as a qualifying subject. Degrees such as Environmental Science, Biomedical Science, Health Science, Food Science, Sports Science and Forensic Science would fit into this category.

A degree in Science?

The nature of the course will dictate the kind of modules studied but whatever the course there will usually be some compulsory modules in the first year and some specialised options in the last two years.

Combining Science with other degree subjects

Science-related degrees are often combined with a whole range of subjects at university level. But the most common subjects that are studied jointly with Science include Maths, IT/Computing, Philosophy, Business/Management and sometimes a modern language.

Foundation degrees and Diplomas

There are many different science Foundation courses available, and they tend to specialise in particular areas such as animal science or bioscience. There are also BTEC Higher Nationals on offer in Applied Science.

Science and your future career

Applied Science can set you up for particular career pathways in Science such as working in scientific analysis, the environment, manufacturing, healthcare and electronics. In many cases, further study is required to work in scientific roles. Nevertheless, Science is still a good subject to prepare you for entry level jobs in many sectors of work including non-science areas such as commerce and public sector.

Degree options for Science graduates really depend on the particular course studied. For career options, look under jobs sections for the A levels in Biology, Chemistry, Physics and Environmental Science in this guide and you will see that there are many possible opportunities for Science graduates.

Further information

Forensic Science Society	www.forensic-science-society.org.uk
Institute of Biology	www.iob.org
Institute of Biomedical Sciences	www.ibms.org
Institute of Physics	www.iop.org
NHS Careers	www.nhscareers.nhs.uk
Royal Society of Chemistry	www.chemsoc.org

SOCIOLOGY

Sociology is the scientific study of society. It is about all kinds of social relationships that people share with each other; in their families, in their schools and in work. The course concentrates on choice of family, the mass media, health and welfare policy, education, work and training and the study of the law and crime. As an A level sociologist, you will learn some of the methods used by sociologists and apply your knowledge to the study of a topic of your own choice to produce an individual piece of research for examination.

Subject options

This subject is available at GCE A/AS level.

A/AS level

For an exact definition of the AS and A2 syllabus you will be studying, you should consult your school, college or the exam board itself. The following outline is based largely on the AQA syllabus.

- Unit 1: culture and identity; families and households; wealth, poverty and welfare
- Unit 2: education; health; sociological methods
- Unit 3: beliefs and society; global development; mass media; power and politics
- Unit 4: crime and deviance; stratification and differentiation; theory and methods.

AS students complete units one and two; A2 students complete units one to four. Assessment is by written exams.

How is A/AS level Sociology taught and assessed?

There is a lot of reading and writing in this subject and much consideration of contemporary political and social issues. No prior knowledge is needed but an interest in the issues is important. You may look at government policies, newspaper reports, films and social documentaries to bolster your knowledge. Assessment is by a combination of coursework and written exams.

Choosing other subjects to go with Sociology

This could be combined with Arts or Science subjects. Social Policy, Politics/Government, Health and Social Care and Economics would all go well. Always be careful there isn't too much of an overlap between your subjects though.

Sociology at HE level

Sociology at a higher level will go into much more depth than it was possible at A level and you will develop many more critical approaches with which to analyse the issues. Often Sociology is associated with Social Policy at a departmental level within universities even though they are different subjects. Institutions do not normally require A level Sociology to study it at degree level.

A degree in Sociology?

There are many different kinds of degrees in this area. As well as Social Policy and Sociology, universities sometimes offer a Social Science degree which covers both of these subjects and a bit more! Some of the modules you might find on a three-year Sociology BA include:

- Deviance, crime and social control
- Identity, difference and inequalities
- Introduction to race and ethnicity
- Key debates in sociology
- Research methods
- Sociological thinking
- Sociological analysis of contemporary society
- Stigma deviance and society.

Combining Sociology with other degree subjects

This subject obviously goes well with Social Policy but other possible complementary subjects include Politics, Economics, Philosophy, Geography, English and History.

Foundation degrees and Diplomas

There are some related Foundation degrees but they tend to be focused on specific aspects of Social Policy or Sociology such as Criminology. There are no BTEC Higher Nationals currently on offer in this area.

Sociology and your future career

Non-graduate jobs

Sociology will enable you, along with your other subjects, to get junior positions in many areas of business, the public sector and the not-for-profit sector. Jobs in Sociology would be hard to find without a degree but getting an administrative position in Social Services, Prison Service, or in a Non-Governmental Organisation (NGO) would be a possibility.

Graduate jobs related to Sociology

- **Education, teaching and lecturing:** this can be at secondary level, where a PGCE is required, or in Further or Higher Education.

- **Probation officer:** provides a social work service to all the courts. Work involves the supervision of offenders in the community, the care of offenders in custody and the aftercare of released offenders.
- **Social/community work:** this includes social work and community work, careers and educational guidance and counselling roles.
- **Social research:** this could mean working for a local authority, charity/ campaign organisation, trade union, political party or as a parliamentary research assistant at Westminster.
- **Social worker:** supports people who need help or protection. Work is done with children and families but also with those coping with issues such as homelessness, addictions and mental health problems.

Graduate jobs where a degree in Sociology could be useful

- **Counsellor:** works with individuals and sometimes with groups, in confidence, to explore dissatisfaction or distress. A counsellor will aim to enable someone to overcome personal difficulties and facilitate change.
- **Housing manager:** develops, supplies and manages housing for local authorities and housing associations.
- **Prison governor:** plans, organises and co-ordinates, in accordance with Home Office policies, the activities and resources necessary for the efficient running of a prison.
- **Welfare rights adviser:** concerned with giving information and advice to members of the public on matters which are usually of a legal or financial nature and affecting the individual's rights and basic welfare.

Further information

Social Work Careers	www.socialworkcareers.co.uk
Sociology website	www.sociology.org.uk
Sociology revision website	www.sociologystuff.com

TRAVEL AND TOURISM

The global travel and tourism industry is still booming. This means the demand for well qualified staff is high. As a student of this course, you will improve your knowledge, understanding and skills related to the vocational area of travel and tourism. It will also give you a good platform from which to study this subject further. As well as giving you a good background in this area, you can also choose to focus on particular career areas such as Marketing, Customer Service, World Wide Travel Destinations and Tourism Development, as well as providing an appreciation of the wider Travel and Tourism environment.

Subject options

This subject is available as a GCE A/AS level and as BTEC National qualifications. From September 2010, a new Advanced Diploma in Travel and Tourism will also be available.

A/AS level

The exam boards offer this course and cover very similar ground in terms of content. The main variations are in terms of module names and how the options are organised. For an exact definition of the AS and A2 syllabus you will be studying, you should consult your school, college or the exam board itself. The following outline is based largely on the OCR syllabus.

Unit no.	Unit title	Unit no.	Unit title
1	Introducing travel and tourism	9	Tourism development
2	Customer service in travel and tourism	10	Event management
3	Travel destinations	11	The guided tour
4	International travel	12	Ecotourism
5	Tourist attractions	13	Adventure tourism
6	Organising travel	14	Culture tourism
7	Hospitality	15	Marketing in travel and tourism
8	Working overseas	16	Human resources in travel and tourism

This course is available as a single or double award, at both AS and A level.

You need no prior knowledge of this subject to take the course, however, and interest in the topic as well as career motivation in this area are advantages. As well as classroom work, students may visit different types of travel and tourism organisations, and do lots of independent research about the sector. Assessment is by a combination of externally set and marked written exams and internally assessed portfolios of evidence.

BTEC Nationals

These qualifications are aimed to give students the practical skills needed by the job market in that particular sector. BTEC Nationals are available in three levels (Award, Certificate and Diploma).

The following options are available at Award, Certificate and Diploma level:

- Aviation Operations
- Travel and Tourism.

Choosing other subjects to go with Travel and Tourism

This subject goes well with other applied subjects such as Leisure Studies and Applied Business. (Check in case there may be too much overlap and exam boards may not permit the combination.) Equally, it would go well with GCE A levels in Business, Accounting and a foreign language.

Travel and Tourism at HE level

There are different types of courses in this area. There are a few degree courses such as Travel and Tourism Management but there are also many options at Foundation degree Level and at BTEC Higher National level. Some degree courses are sandwich courses, meaning that students work for a year in the travel and tourism industry and some point during their course. Some courses offer a year abroad option. You don't necessarily need to have studied this subject previously to be accepted onto a degree course.

A degree in Travel and Tourism?

A sample of modules that a BA (Hons) degree in this subject might look like the following:

- Adventure tourism
- E-tourism
- Global tourism issues
- Incoming & domestic tourism
- Marketing and accounting
- Organisational studies
- Tourism today
- Travel agency operations
- Travel trade & IATA studies
- Visitor attraction studies
- World geography or a language (French, German or Spanish).

Combining Travel and Tourism with other degree subjects

This subject goes very well a modern foreign language as well subjects such as Business/Management, Accounting, Geography, as well as Computing/IT.

Foundation degrees and Diplomas

There are many Travel and Tourism Foundation degrees as well as some related to specific areas of the sector. Edexcel offers BTEC Higher Nationals in Travel and Tourism Management.

Travel and Tourism and your future career

Non-graduate jobs

This sector is always crying out for people so it's a bit easier for students to get jobs straight after A levels. Trainee positions do exist with travel companies, agencies and tour operators as well as with some airlines.

Graduate jobs directly related to Travel and Tourism

- **Holiday rep:** employed in resorts to look after holidaymakers, includes children's reps and administrators. Work is hard and demanding, usually working on rota systems.
- **Tour manager:** travels with groups of holidaymakers on package tours at home and overseas.
- **Tourism officer:** develops and promotes a quality tourism product which will attract visitors and produce significant economic benefits for a country or region.
- **Tourist information centre manager:** provides information to visitors to the area and sells guidebooks, maps and products.
- **Travel agent:** acts as a link between the client and tour operator. They are responsible for advising customers and selling travel services.

Graduate jobs where a degree in Travel and Tourism could be useful

- **Arts administrator:** responsible for managing the theatre/gallery, etc., managing financial resources, marketing and attracting sponsorship to support the arts.
- **Event organiser:** identifies potential business, researches, writes, plans and runs all aspects of conferences or exhibitions on behalf of a client or own organisation.
- **Hotel manager:** manages hotel, restaurant, etc. whilst promoting facilities and services, organising special events and recruiting staff.
- **Public relations officer:** writes press releases, produces publicity brochures and promotional literature (may work in conjunction with marketing dept), produces customer/staff newspapers and magazines.

Further information

The Association of British Travel Agents (ABTA)	www.abta.com
The Institute of Travel and Tourism	www.itt.co.uk
Travel Industry Jobs website	www.travelindustryjobs.co.uk

PART THREE

EXAMS AND BEYOND

Making a success of your studies – revision tips

In this section you will:

- *find out how you learn effectively*
- *learn how to prepare effectively for exams*
- *discover how exam boards assess students' work*
- *think about ways of improving your exam technique.*

How do you learn best?

Having made the choices about *what* you're going to study, your main focus will probably shift to *how* you're going to study! There are many different ways of studying and revising and you need to find methods that work best for you. In reality, your teacher or tutor will use different methods to take account for the fact that people learn in different ways. But do you know how you learn best? Do you know why some activities appeal to you and some don't?

There has been lots of research about this and lots of theories developed, but a very simple one is shown in the table below. Are you someone who learns best my seeing or visualising things (visual learner)? Or do remember by what you hear (auditory)? Or are you a hands-on practical learner, someone who needs to feel and touch things (kinaesthetic)? Look at the questions on the left and put a tick or a cross next to the one(s) which apply to you most (more than one statement may be true for you for each question). Then total up your ticks at the end.

	Visual	**Auditory**	**Kinaesthetic/Tactile**
When I try to spell a word I...	try to see to see the word in my mind's eye	say the word aloud to see what it sounds like	write the word down to find out if it feels right
When I'm having a conversation I...	don't like listening for too long. I tend do use words such as 'see', 'picture', 'imagine'	enjoy listening but am impatient to talk. I use words such as 'hear' and 'it sounds like'	gesture and use expressive movements. I use words such as 'feel', 'touch' and 'hold'
When I'm concentrating I...	become distracted by untidiness or movements	become distracted by sounds or noises	by activity around me

When I've met someone once before I...	can't remember their name but remember their face	can't remember what they look like, but remember their name and what was talked about	remember best what we did together
When I'm trying to contact someone I...	prefer to see them face-to-face	prefer to use the telephone	prefer to talk to them while walking or engaging in an activity
When I read a book I...	enjoy descriptive scenes and vivid imagery	enjoy the dialogue and conversation between characters	prefer action stories (or don't enjoy it because I'm not a keen reader)
When I'm learning things, I...	like to see demonstrations, diagrams, slides, or posters	prefer verbal instructions or talking about it with someone else	prefer to try and do it myself if possible and 'get stuck in'
Totals			

Adapted from Colin Rose, *Accelerated Learning* (Accelerated Learning Systems Ltd., Aylesbury Bucks. Tel: 01296 631177)

Some people have a very strong preference for one way of doing things; others are more of a mixture of all three. Whatever your preference, it's important to think about this (as well as any other insights about the way you take in and remember information best) when you're thinking about the best ways to study and revise. For instance, look at the following examples showing how you can use this information to improve your learning ability:

Situation: *You can't understand something your teacher is trying to explain*

Options: *Ask politely if he or she could write it down or put it in a diagram. Or try and draw it yourself.*

Situation: *You can't seem to remember much by looking over your revision notes*

Options: *Record your notes on tape and listen to them or get someone to test you and make a game out of it!*

These are just two examples of how doing things in a different way can make it much easier for you to learn and therefore enjoy the subject.

Your strategy for success

As well as taking into account how your brain works best, there are lots of other practical things you can do to make studies as successful as possible. Success at this level really comes down to four things: being organised, understanding what the exam board wants, revision and exam technique. Let's look at each in turn.

Get organised!

As soon as you start school or college for your post-16 qualifications you will be given a timetable. Unlike GCSE study where all your time is accounted for at school, at this stage you will probably have periods where you don't have any lessons. From this official timetable, you could build in your own personal timetable taking into account the following:

- Time for independent study or revision
- Time for socialising
- Time for part-time work (if you have to do it)
- Time doing nothing!

For each subject you are studying, your tutor will give you an idea of how much independent reading around the subject is required to get a good grade. Once you get this information, you will be able to build it into your timetable.

Other simple ways of staying organised include:

- Keeping a notebook of things to do so you don't forget
- Not taking on too much work outside studies
- Getting into the habit of doing things straight away rather than leaving them (if possible)
- Keeping daily lists of things to do.

Effective note-taking is very important for study at this level too. You might not have time to write down every single word your teacher says on a subject, but try and get into the habit of recording at least the key information. Remember that you will have to do a lot of note-taking at home as well, when you are reading around the subject.

Understanding what the exam boards want

How A levels, AS levels and equivalents are assessed varies from subject to subject, but there are many elements that are common to all of them. They are outlined below.

Skills

These days syllabuses are called specifications. This is because you are being assessed on the skills you've developed as well as the knowledge you've acquired. Both examinations and coursework test a number of subject-based skills such as planning and experimental skills in Science and reading and listening in Modern Languages.

Spiritual, moral, ethical, cultural and other issues

Students are also supposed to show an awareness of these issues in relation to what they are studying. Mentioning these issues, where relevant, in coursework and exams will probably help your cause.

Coursework

As well as written exams, many subjects have an element of coursework. For some subjects this is a lot; in others, very little. Examiners look for the same kinds of skills that they would in written exams although there may be different criteria applied for some subjects. Coursework is marked by your class teacher and a sample of the work is sent to the exam board to be moderated. Sometimes this is marked down by the moderator, so bear in mind that the mark that your teacher gives you is not necessarily the final mark!

Grading and grade boundaries

Grade boundaries are set each year once all the marks are in and they vary from year to year. In reality, what this means is that someone may get a grade A one year with a certain standard of work, and the following year another person might get a grade B for the same standard of work. It seems unfair, but that's the way the system works. Having said that, the descriptions of grades are pretty much standard, and it's quite clear what's of a very good standard and what's of an average standard. Take this example below, which is a definition of Grades, A, C and E in relation to A level Law (AQA Exam board):

- **Grade A** Candidates are able to recall a substantial body of relevant information and present a well-structured response to the question, identifying a range of issues. They are able consistently to integrate descriptive and evaluative material, make connections where appropriate, demonstrate strong analytical and problem-solving skills and conduct a sound, coherent and relevant argument, supported appropriately.
- **Grade C** Candidates recall a sound body of information and are able to relate it to issues raised by the questions. They demonstrate some analytical and problem-solving skills, make connections and present a sound argument with some use of authority or other evidence.
- **Grade E** Candidates either provide generally accurate accounts of some relevant, descriptive material and/or identify issues raised by the question, identify connections and offer a basic evaluation drawing simple conclusions.

Applied A/AS level subjects

In general, applied subjects contain a much lower element of written exams. Instead, emphasis is placed on building up a portfolio of evidence. This could include a case study, a report, some practical work (e.g. something you've created), or anything else. These are often internally assessed and externally moderated, but some elements of the applied courses are also assessed by external examiners.

Revision technique

There are many ways to revise, and different things work for different people. Look at the following list of tips and see what works best for you.

- Just as you created a timetable for study, you should also draw up a revision timetable. Work out when your exams are and calculate how much time you need to revise thoroughly for each one. Don't leave this too late or too near to the start of your exams.
- Know where your exams are and when they start, how long they are and what equipment you are allowed to take in (calculators, etc.) and what you are not allowed to take in (mobiles phones, etc.).
- Make sure you have one weekend day when you don't do revision or think about exams – you'll come back to it refreshed.
- Start off revising your subjects with everything you need to know on a piece of paper. Then, as you keep revising it, reduce it down to the key points and the stuff you can't remember. Gradually, you should be able to get all your revision key points onto a postcard!
- Some people (auditory people!) revise well by listening, so 'talk' their revision onto cassette tapes and then listen to these while lying in bed, while travelling in a car or walking to the shops (on a personal stereo).
- Having a good diet and enough rest as well as some regular exercise helps keep you energised, focused and optimistic. Have an early night before exams.
- On the morning of the exam, have a good breakfast, stay calm and allow plenty of time to get to the exam and remember that you can only do your best.

Assessment/Examination technique

- Before the exams, have a look at the exam board's specification to see what is required to achieve the different grades as well as looking at any past papers to give you an idea of the types of questions you may be facing.
- In terms of coursework assessment, before you hand in your work, make sure it meets the requirements outlined by your teacher and on the exam board's website if you wish.
- During an exam, work out how much time you've got for each section of the paper and stick to your plan.
- If you have to write an essay during an exam, spend some time at the start of the exam coming up with a plan and structure for the essay. This will keep you on track.
- If you finish the exam early, go back and check over your work. You may not feel like doing this, but it could mean the difference between one grade and another!

Further help

BBC Learning site. Gives revision help not just for A levels and AS levels, but also Scottish Highers and Welsh Exams — www.bbc.co.uk/learning/subjects/schools.shtml

Examzone (a site hosted by Edexcel) — www.examzone.co.uk

The Student Room (online forum for students to share exam experiences, help with revision, etc.) — www.thestudentroom.co.uk

T. Buzan, *Use your Head* (BBC Active)

Endnote: what next?

In this section you will find out a bit more about some of the options open to you after your Level 3 qualifications.

Decisions, decisions! Once you've chosen your Level 3 qualifications, it won't be long before you have to think about what to do afterwards. HE is an obvious choice for many, but it's not the only thing on offer. Here are some of the options.

Higher/Further Education

There are a number of options here including:

- **An academic degree** such as Maths, Physics, English, History, Modern Languages and so on. These courses usually last three years, sometimes four. This is still the most popular option in terms of Higher Education and remains the gateway for many of the higher-salaried jobs. For more detailed information see the section on HE options for each of the corresponding A level entries. You can also search for a course at www.ucas.com.
- **A vocational degree** such as Medicine, Engineering, Dentistry, Nursing and so on. These courses often take longer than three years and sometimes include on the job experience as part of the qualification.
- **A sandwich/industrial degree.** subjects such as Business studies, Engineering, IT Computing, Retail Management and so on. These are courses which include a year's placement in a relevant industry.
- **A Foundation degree.** These are offered in the whole range of subjects but are usually vocationally based and include work experience. They last two years and can be converted to a full degree. Search for them at www.ucas.com.
- **A BTEC Higher National Diploma (HND).** These are similar to Foundation degrees in that they tend to be vocationally-based and can be converted to Diplomas or full degrees. Unlike Foundation degrees, however, they hold more recognition with employers, partly because they have been around for a much longer time.

All of the above can be taken on a full-time or part-time basis and subjects in some instances may be studied alone or jointly with other subjects (e.g. French with History).

Straight into employment

It's a fact that more and more jobs can only be accessed by those who've been through Higher Education. However, there are still many areas of work where it's possible to climb the ladder from a Level 3 qualification such as A levels, Scottish Highers or equivalents. These include:

- **Some areas of retail**. Many organisations (such as the Arcadia Group) in this sector offer specific training schemes for Level 3-qualified students who don't want to do Higher Education.
- **Journalism and the media**. Some local newspapers still take on school leavers and train them up. This is how many top journalists started their profession.
- **Travel, tourism and the airline business**. It's possible to get started with airlines (maybe as a cabin crew member) or in the travel business which has specific schemes. An applied A level in Travel and Tourism might help.
- **Sales**. If you can sell, that's all that counts. It doesn't matter if you have a degree or not.
- **Civil Service/local government**. As an A level/equivalent student, it's possible to get junior administrative positions in this sector and then work your way up.
- **Leisure and recreation**. Jobs in sports centres, health and fitness clubs, as personal trainers are all possible without a degree.

These are just some of the work-related options and there be many more. Speak to your school careers adviser if you have one or your Connexions adviser for further guidance.

Graduate employment

It is estimated that about 60 per cent of graduate jobs are open to students irrespective of their degree subject. What tends to interest employers most are previous experience as well as skills, potential and personal qualities. It's important to get involved in outside activities while you're a student so that the whole range of employers will be interested in your portfolio of skills and abilities.

Taking time out before employment or further study

This is a very common option. It may be that you need some time to think before making your next move, it could be that you need a break from studying, or it could be that you want to get some work experience before going to further study. From an employer's point of view, or from the viewpoint of university admissions department, it's not a problem at all, so long as you can show that you've done something worthwhile with the time. Some of the gap-year options include:

- Getting some work experience, perhaps in an area that might move into later
- Travel abroad to broaden your horizons

- Do some charity/voluntary work overseas (such as VSO)
- Teach English abroad
- A combination of the above!

If you approach it in the right way, and don't spend the whole year lying on a beach somewhere, then taking a year out can really add to your skills, develop your maturity, and generally make you more employable.

Whatever you decide to do, always try to focus on why you're doing it, where it's leading and whether you're going to enjoy it. With these three things in mind, you should make good decisions throughout your life. I wish you well.

Further information

Connexions website (Lots of information about post-16 and post-18 choices)	www.connexions-direct.com
Edexcel website (You can search for BTEC Nationals)	www.edexcel.org.uk
Gap year website	www.yearoutgroup.org
UCAS website (You can search for full degrees and Foundation degrees)	www.ucas.com

Useful contacts and sources of further information

Qualifications and Curriculum Authority

QCA Customer Relations
83 Piccadilly
London
W1J 8QA
Enquiries: 020 7509 5556
www.qca.org.uk

Exam Boards

AQA	CCEA	EDEXCEL
Stag Hill House	29 Clarendon Road	One90 High Holborn
Guildford	Clarendon Dock	London
Surrey	Belfast	WC1V 7BH
GU2 7XJ	BT1 3BG	Tel: 020 7190 5700
Tel: 01483 506506	Tel: 028 9026 1200	www.edexcel.org.uk
www.aqa.org.uk	www.ccea.org.uk	
OCR	**WJEC**	
1 Hills Road	245 Western Avenue	
Cambridge	Cardiff	
CB1 2EU	CF5 2YX	
Tel: 01223 553998	Tel: 029 2026 5000	
www.ocr.org.uk	www.wjec.co.uk	